T0246321

IN THE GHOST SHADOWS

IN THE GHOST SHADOWS

THE UNTOLD STORY OF CHINATOWN'S MOST POWERFUL CRIME BOSS

PETER CHIN
WITH EVERETT De MORIER

CITADEL PRESS
Kensington Publishing Corp.
kensingtonbooks.com

CITADEL PRESS BOOKS are published by

Kensington Publishing Corp.
900 Third Avenue
New York, NY 10022

All Kensington titles, imprints, and distributed lines are available at special quantity discounts for bulk purchases for sales promotions, premiums, fund-raising, educational, or institutional use. Special book excerpts or customized printings can also be created to fit specific needs. For details, write or phone the office of the Kensington sales manager: Kensington Publishing Corp., 900 Third Avenue, New York, NY 10022, attn Sales Department; phone 1-800-221-2647.

CITADEL PRESS and the Citadel logo are Reg. U.S. Pat. & TM Off.

10 9 8 7 6 5 4 3 2 1

First Citadel hardcover printing: February 2025

Printed in the United States of America

ISBN: 978-0-8065-4385-7

ISBN: 978-0-8065-4387-1 (e-book)

Library of Congress Control Number: 2024944364

Peter Chin would like to dedicate this book to his loving mother and wonderful sisters.

CONTENTS

FOREWORD
By S. J. Peddie

Chinatown, New York City. A tourist mecca and seemingly impenetrable community. Behind the cheap trinkets and souvenirs, there's a feeling of a deep undercurrent, of an entire world beneath the shiny surface. But the language barrier, obscure customs, and a deep distrust of outsiders make it nearly impossible to comprehend.

Enter Peter Chin. He was an immigrant in a poor and struggling family from Hong Kong. A natural leader, his life might have been different, but for one thing: his violent and abusive father. His father's temper was so explosive that Chin was afraid to even cough in his presence.

Unable to protect his mother and sisters, or himself, Chin fled to the streets as a mere thirteen-year-old. With just $5 in his pocket and no food, he learned to survive and thrive, according to the rough code of Chinatown's underworld.

It is through his vivid memories of his life on the streets that we learn about Chinatown's criminal underside. He and coauthor Everett De Morier lift the veil on the secret world of Chinese organized crime. From the colorful nicknames, like Applehead, Mongo, and Stinky Bug, to the secret rituals, like the gangster induction ceremony, it is a rare opportunity to understand its inner workings and reach.

It's not easy to get gangsters to talk. After all, they live by a code of silence. They rarely talk about their lives to civilians, much less writers. De Morier showed resourcefulness and tenacity in getting Chin to tell his story. He credits Mike Moy, a retired Chinese cop, for opening the door for him and persuading Chin to talk. Moy didn't care about money or credit—he cared about preserving history. This book does just that.

Anyone who thinks criminals don't follow the news coverage about them is dead wrong. They follow it avidly. That's how Chin's gang came by their name. A newspaper reporter had written a story about their crimes and concluded with a bit of a poetic flourish:

They came in like a shadow and left without a trace . . . like a ghost shadow.

The gang loved it. From then on, they called themselves the Ghost Shadows.

As Kid Jai, the name he was called in a sign of respect, Chin built the Ghost Shadows into the most powerful gang in Chinatown. He traveled the world and dealt with all levels of people. There were trips to San Francisco, Toronto, and Hong Kong. He negotiated business deals with millionaires and once persuaded kidnappers to release a terrified movie star a rival gang was holding hostage. Chin's power and influence extended far beyond the confines of Chinatown.

At one point, he had the opportunity to get more involved in the highly lucrative world of entertainment. Initially, it seemed like a good opportunity. But he found the stars and their entourages too demanding and needy. He couldn't take it. He got out of that.

His experience illustrates a truism of organized crime: It's everywhere. It's not just in the gambling dens or internet sex trafficking—it's in the so-called legitimate businesses of society. Gangsters know that's where the real money is.

The reach of organized crime is something few people truly understand. Whether it's Chinese, Italian, Albanian, Russian, or Mexican, organized crime is a threat because it is simply that: *organized.* These criminal groups talk to each other and do business together. Though they have their own rules and relationships, the smart ones—leaders like Chin—understand that cooperation makes them richer.

Chin shrewdly struck up a business relationship with a high-ranking member of the Genovese crime family, and they made a fortune off their loan-sharking arrangement. In prison, he was a regular handball partner of Sonny Franzese, underboss of the Colombo crime family. As secretive and insular as organized crime groups and families can be, men like Chin and Franzese understood each other.

Both Chin and Franzese got caught up in the war waged against organized crime by law enforcement from the 1960s through the 1980s. By then, even FBI Director J. Edgar Hoover, who had long denied the existence of organized crime, had to confront the reality of its power and influence. The government recruited FBI agents and cops. By 1970, Congress had passed RICO, the Racketeer Influenced and Corrupt Organizations Act. The law made it easier to charge gangsters because it allowed federal prosecutors to focus on criminal behavior, as opposed to a single criminal act. It also provided for stiffer sentences and seizure of criminal assets. Armed with motivated agents and cops, as well as the devastating legal weapon of RICO in the courtroom, prosecutors set out to crush organized crime.

They didn't. To be sure, they sent a lot of guys away to prison for a long time. Chin served more than twenty years. Franzese, close to thirty. Prosecutors also managed to flip many criminals who were loath to spend long stretches behind bars. But the lure of fast money and power is simply too great, and the acquiescence of politicians chasing the same money and power is too easy. Organized crime has not gone away. It lurks still in the shadows. Wherever there is an opportunity to make money, it's there.

For immigrants like Chin and Franzese, organized crime offers something more: community and a sense of family. It is difficult to overstate how disorienting moving to another country—one with a completely different set of rules and traditions—can be. When there's the challenge of learning a new language, or as in Chin's case, the lack of a basic education, it can be even more isolating.

In my years of investigative reporting, I've been struck how strong the bonds of organized crime are. There's a camaraderie, an understanding, and even forgiveness among guys who might have tried to kill one another at another time. De Morier was struck by that as well. After spending more than two years getting to know Chin and unspooling his story and the violence that he endured, De Morier was amazed by Chin's capacity for forgiveness. Chin was able to forgive everyone—except his own father.

As a reader and journalist, I'm always interested in how the writer feels about the subject. De Morier wisely shares his observations. When he first met Chin, he writes, "My first impression of Kid Jai was that he was not what I expected of an organized crime boss. Peter was boisterous and funny, personable, gregarious."

That sounds exactly right. Franzese was the same way— funny, smart, and a great storyteller. And even though he was more than 100 years old and hobbled by physical infirmities when I first met him, he was a flirt.

I remember mentioning my impressions of Franzese to a prosecutor who had chased a number of high-profile mobsters throughout his career. He wasn't surprised. He pointed out that leaders of all kinds—from corporate CEOS to Mob bosses—all had to have charismatic personalities to get people to follow them.

And follow them they did. Both Chin and Franzese inspired loyalty among the men who worked for them. That's not always the case. Mob guys resented Mob boss Joe Profaci for "taxing" them for more and more money and for giving choice positions to family members. They sneered at Profaci's successor, Joseph Magliocco, because he wasn't a tough guy. They came to despise Paul Castellano because he was too greedy.

With Chin and Franzese, however, that wasn't the case. They let their guys make money, and they formed genuine friendships with them. Both were wily and lucky enough to avoid getting killed. Had they not been interrupted by law enforcement, both likely would have continued to build their criminal enterprises.

In Chin's case, the interruption came in 1985. That's when the federal government launched the largest mass Asian racketeering case in US history. He was one of twenty-five Chinese gangsters charged with racketeering, including crimes such as extortion, robbery, and kidnapping spanning a decade. Rudolph Giuliani, then the US Attorney for the Southern District of New York, announced the indictment.

Chin was convicted, and upon going to prison, told his wife to divorce him. He wanted to free her of the burden of being married to him. Once he was in prison, he decided to make the best of it. He, of course, managed to make money off some illicit gambling behind bars—but he also spent his time on something far more important. Thanks to another inmate, who patiently spent hours with him, he learned to read and write.

Perhaps that's what got him thinking about changing his life. Or maybe it was the years of confinement. Or it could have simply been a sort of wisdom that comes with age. Whatever it was, Chin decided to get out.

When he was released from prison, he left the underworld behind. He got his first legitimate job at the age of forty-six. Navigating his entry into a different world after prison wasn't easy, but he had certainly overcome bigger challenges. Although many things had changed, he still followed the news avidly.

Chin laughed when he learned that his nemesis in the courtroom, Giuliani, had been charged with racketeering under the RICO law for his alleged role in overturning the 2020 election.

He didn't feel revenge or anger. He relished the irony of it.

Throughout his life, Chin has managed to avoid bitterness

and see the humor in many of the situations he's faced. And with the help of De Morier, who describes himself as a "naïve but fascinated" observer, he has preserved an important piece of history and opened a window onto a little-known world for the rest of us.

It's well worth a look.

S. J. Peddie is an award-winning investigative journalist and the author of Sonny: The Last of the Old-Time Mafia Bosses, John "Sonny" Franzese.

An Unlikely Friendship
By Everett De Morier

This is Peter Chin's story, but to really understand it, you need to hear Mike Moy's story, because everything begins with him. That's how this book came to be.

From age sixteen until he turned twenty-four, Mike Moy spent his time in a New York Chinatown street gang known as the Fuk Ching. His job was simple: robbery, extortion, fighting, and just plain surviving. Most people who take this path find themselves at an abrupt end, either by death or by incarceration. Mike chose an unusual path—he switched sides by attending and graduating from the police academy and joining the NYPD.

Mike Moy went from criminal to cop, and for the next nine years he patrolled the same Chinatown streets he once extorted as a criminal.

This illustrates the division of two lives, the crook and the cop, and occasionally those worlds crossed. One day, while on patrol in 2001, Mike ran into a childhood friend.

Kenny Wong had previously been a member of the Ghost Shadows, once the most powerful organized crime group in Chinatown. Though both men had committed many crimes together in their youth, they now resided in a transitional period of their lives—Mike's as a cop and Kenny's as a free man just released from federal prison. After a brief cordial exchange, the two promised to stay in touch. A few months later, when the Twin Towers were attacked, Mike was one of the first responders, which took priority over catching up with Kenny.

In 2004, after nine years as a patrolman with the NYPD, Mike Moy was promoted to detective, and he spent the next seventeen years investigating crimes in Chinatown. He spent two of those years on the Asian Hate Crime Task Force.

I knew the basics about Mike Moy's story when we first started talking in 2016 about the possibility of my writing his memoir. We decided to discuss it over lunch in Staten Island, the halfway point between Mike's Bensonhurst, Brooklyn, home and mine in Dover, Delaware.

The lunch went well, we connected, and it looked like this project would move forward. What I didn't know then, and wouldn't know until years later, is that one minor error on my part blew the deal. Mike and I walked out of the restaurant, shook hands, and headed to our cars. Only my car was parked a few blocks away, while Mike's was right across the street. That detail stopped everything for Mike. The opportunity evaporated for me because, for a street guy like Mike, a man trained to value trust and instinct, he now had questions.

What is he hiding? With plenty of places to park in front of the restaurant, why did he park so far away? Did he not want me to see his car? What does he not want me to know about him?

In reality, my parking location was dictated by the fact that in the Staten Island traffic, I missed my turn and couldn't get back to it. I parked a few blocks up and walked back.

In the weeks that followed, the communication between Mike and me slowed down, then dwindled to a stop.

From a typical American standpoint, where you park your car seems like a small detail on which to base a major decision. An insignificant footnote. But most choices on the streets of Chinatown are based on trust. If you trust someone with your secrets, you are trusting them with your life.

In the early twentieth century, Chinese immigrants came in large numbers to New York's Lower East Side, the place that would eventually become Chinatown. The new arrivals could live and work there, raise families, build businesses, join organizations, all without needing to speak or read English. Because of this, the rules, norms, and cultures of Chinatown became all the rules and norms a person needed. That misty area beyond Mott and Pell Streets became its own small world.

In fact, they had a general mistrust for the world outside Chinatown. Early in the twentieth century, raids driven by anti-Chinese mobs were not uncommon, leading to the destruction of personal property and even murder. Chinatown created a familiar home, and the tongs created the government within that new home. These tongs began as civil organizations that settled disputes and helped people get job training and placement for the manufacturing opportunities in Chinatown, as well as loans for businesses.

Unfortunately, this quickly morphed into criminal organizations, taking bribes, extorting, and profiting from illegal activities such as gambling, opium, and prostitution. The tongs became the governing force of Chinatown.

In 1906, much of San Francisco's Chinatown population migrated to New York's Chinatown after a 7.9-magnitude earthquake devastated San Francisco and left half the residents without homes.

Think about this for a moment: A large group of Chinese immigrants, lured from China with the promise of railroad jobs and the gold rush, traveled three thousand miles from the West to the East Coast in order to live in another small part of a major city. They would have passed by a myriad of livable towns and cities before getting to New York. To be in a place where they would be comfortable. Where they would be safe. To a world they knew.

Chinatown continued to grow and then exploded as the 1965 Immigration Act made it easier than ever before for immigrants from China to enter the United States. With this rapid population influx the tongs' influence grew, as did the need to control that power through the muscle of organized street gangs.

Chinatown continued this way—with the tongs and organized crime groups in charge—for many years. In fact, it has only been in the last decade that the final vestiges of this world have completely faded.

After nine years as a uniformed patrol officer and seventeen years as an NYPD detective, Mike Moy retired after twenty-six years in July of 2021 and began to reflect on what the next chapter of his life should be.

The events of 9/11 changed many things for many people. Mike watched friends, other cops, and first responders he had served with die because of lingering health issues from that day. Mike also has health issues that will most likely shorten his life. This prompted him to think about what is important. Many stories covered 9/11 but not one story covered the *true* history of Chinatown organized crime, largely because several of the key players were incarcerated, had emigrated, or were fugitives.

The peak time of New York's Chinatown, from the 1960s through the 1980s, has never been fully told. After a crime or shooting in Chinatown, reporters were often unable to interview locals because of the language barrier. The NYPD didn't have a Chinese translator on staff, so any material had to be sent to Washington, DC, to be translated.

Reporters relied on the police as their sole source, and Mike knew they filtered the information provided to protect the integrity of the case. Plus, after seventeen years as a Chinatown detective, he was aware that the public stories of the major organized crime events in Chinatown were not the true ones. The criminal subjects mentioned in these articles often didn't read or speak English and, therefore, couldn't comment on media errors. Many of them didn't even know these articles existed until decades later, long after the pieces ran and were then relied upon as references for further media pieces. The cycle went on.

In addition to this was the inherent challenge of a community that held its secrets close. Low-level members of Chinese organized crime rarely broke the code of silence, and high-ranking ones never did. This means that the *real* story from inside the Chinatown Mob, what actually happened, the whens and whys, has never been told.

Mike also knew that the adage "What we don't learn from history, we repeat again" could apply to Chinatown. Might Chinatown eventually revert to its old, violent, and corrupt ways?

Mike Moy wondered if he was the only one interested in this true history of the Chinatown Mob. He decided to find out.

With his newfound free time, Mike traveled to Hong Kong, Vietnam, Mainland China, Cambodia, and Guyana, utilizing street contacts and a private investigator to track down former New York Chinatown gangsters. He filmed them for his planned YouTube channel *Chinatown Gang Stories* as they told their tales for the very first time.

When Mike returned home with all this raw footage, he reached out to his old friend Kenny Wong to interview him. Kenny's conversation became the first one posted on Mike's *Chinatown Gang Stories*. The response was overwhelming. Viewers loved Kenny's honesty and openness as he talked for the first time about the decisions he made and the reasons he took the path he did.

Off camera, Kenny talked reverently and often about his *uncle*, a term of respect used for an older Chinese man.

Kenny told Mike, "If you want to hear the truth about all that happened in Chinatown behind closed doors, stuff about Uncle Benny, the Godfather of Chinatown, and the wars between the Flying Dragons and the Ghost Shadows, you need to talk to Kid Jai."

Kid Jai's (pronounced *kih-jie*) real name was Peter Chin. He acted as the Dai Lo, or boss, of the Ghost Shadows in the 1970s and '80s. After being arrested and charged in 1984, Kid Jai served twenty of his thirty-five-year federal RICO sentence and then returned to New York, where he's lived for the past two decades. Mike asked Kenny to see if Peter would meet with him. The answer came back quickly: no.

Mike waited and then had Kenny reach out to Peter in a different way. The answer remained the same. He tried yet another approach, focusing on his honor. No. After five or six times over a six-month period with a new approach each time, the answer always came back the same: no.

Peter was not going to meet with a cop.

Mike began to think. He knew that money wasn't the motivator here, but he also knew through Kenny's stories that Peter had a certain set of principles. Mike asked Kenny to deliver one more message to the former Dai Lo.

"We've all made it this far," he said, "and we're all getting old. There's a lot of misinformation out there and our story is an important piece of Chinatown's history. Let's talk. Just talk. Because your story might make a difference to someone."

This time the reaction was slightly different when the message came back: "I'll give you five minutes."

The two men met in an empty parking lot in Queens. Mike had five minutes to plead his case, ending with this closing statement: "We don't have much to leave behind in this world . . . except our story. And we hope our story can touch the right people and help future generations make the right choices."

When the five minutes were up, the two men left, but this time with each other's phone number. Peter Chin agreed to be filmed and interviewed. They met several times and filmed in various hotels, as well as in a warehouse Peter used. Mike quickly saw that Peter not only knew the truth about key moments of Chinatown's criminal history but in many instances had been a key player in them.

This is when the story takes an interesting turn, because not only did Mike quickly realize that Peter's story went way beyond a few YouTube interviews (it was much bigger and way more important than that), but over the course of the next few months, Mike and Peter—the ex-gangster and the ex-cop—became friends.

In 2022, six years after our Staten Island lunch, I heard from Mike Moy again. He told me about his quest to document the true stories of the Chinatown Mob, about his YouTube channel, and a little about Peter Chin. He asked if I would be interested in writing Peter's book.

I got a sense early on of Mike and Peter's friendship without even having met Peter. Mike's protectiveness of Peter demonstrated his fondness and respect for the man. During our meeting, Mike asked questions, then backed off to gauge how I responded to see whether this time I would pass this version of the *where-did-you-park-your-car* test. I was interested in the project but had many questions. I had never worked on a book project involving three different people. Mike explained, "I will be here to help, but the deal you make will be between Peter and you."

This impressed me. Mike was putting this project together for reasons other than financial. He really believed in the importance of this book, which made *me* believe the same. I must have passed that second test, because after several emails and phone calls, Mike set up a Zoom call with the three of us.

In another parking lot in Queens, on Mike's phone in his car, I would have my first conversation with Kid Jai, which would also be my interview for the job of telling his story.

My first impression of Kid Jai was that he was not what I expected of an organized crime boss. Peter was boisterous and funny, personable, gregarious. When my conversation with Peter was over, Mike acted as Peter's spokesperson by telling me that Peter would consider my pitch for the book and that they would get back to me.

A few weeks later, Mike called. My terms were acceptable and, more importantly, Peter had learned to trust Mike, and because Mike now trusted me, Peter did as well. A contract was drawn up, and Peter and I officially became partners.

Mike remained an intricate part of the process. He was there at the beginning of my first two-hour phone interview with Peter. He even brought pastries for Peter as we talked in Mike's car. About twenty minutes into the conversation, he left. I'm guessing because he saw I wasn't going to embarrass myself. When Peter and I got together for the first time for a weekend to interview in Dover, Mike came along. Also the time after that, and when we all walked the streets of Chinatown, too. Now I could see that Mike's guardian role had shifted to something else. He enjoyed Peter's company, and the two men had become good friends.

When I asked Peter when he made the decision to finally trust Mike, he said, "When he took me to his home, and I met his wife. That's when I knew he had nothing to hide and he could be trusted. Whoever thought I'd be friends with a cop?" Peter laughed. "But Mike is very genuine."

The story you are about to read is Peter Chin's story. He pulls no punches. He makes no excuses. If he was there when something important happened in Chinatown—and most of the time he was—he will tell you. If he wasn't, he won't speculate.

You'll not only hear the true story of organized crime in New York's Chinatown but see why many of its participants chose the life they did . . . by seeing why Peter made the choices he did.

CHAPTER 1
A New Country, a New Name

Chin Chit Chuey, who would later be given the American name of Peter Chin, may have been born in a hospital on July 8, 1959, but most likely he was born at the family's small house in the farmland outside of Hong Kong. We'll never know because no official record of his birth exists.

We do know that Peter was born near where his family lived at the time, the region of Hong Kong known as the New Territories. In 1959, this was a large and sparsely populated three hundred square miles of tiny villages and farms between Hong Kong Island and the Kowloon Peninsula. The Chin house consisted of cement blocks held together with clay mortar and a thatched roof. It contained a bucket for a bathroom and a makeshift stove made of scavenged parts, and all water needed to be brought into the house, as no plumbing existed.

The family ate and worked in one room and slept on boards raised off the floor. There weren't enough sleeping boards for everyone, so Peter slept with his mother. His father, a man he would not meet until he was eight years old, lived in Brazil.

Peter's parents, Bark and Kiu, had an extremely short courtship in China years before Peter was born. This consisted of Bark walking past Kiu with his family, pointing to the young girl and saying, "That one." It was an arranged marriage, or what locals called a blind one, and with the deal being made, Kiu was given to Bark as his wife. Once they were married, Kiu gave birth to their first daughter, Maria, before the family found a way to slip out of the People's Republic of China and into Hong Kong. Because of the flood of people fleeing Mainland China from 1945 to 1951, the population of Hong Kong swelled from six hundred thousand to over two million.

Once the Chins were settled in the New Territories, three more daughters were born: Nancy, Mary, and Victoria. It was shortly after Peter was born that Bark would move to Brazil.

It's possible that Bark was working while in Brazil, but the only financial support the Chin family received came from Bark's father, a man named Chow, who sent small but regular checks to his daughter-in-law from the United States, where he and his wife, Kim On, had emigrated.

It was those checks that allowed Kiu to take care of her family and keep them alive. She fed them, cared for them, clothed them, and kept them safe in that small clay house. She was able to occasionally bring in a little extra money by raising and selling the odd pig, doing needlework, or anything else she could do from home.

Life went on for the Chins. Peter's sisters grew old enough to go to school, and then it was Peter's turn to go. Kiu saved enough money for Peter's school uniform, and he was so excited that he couldn't sleep the night before his first day. That morning he got dressed, put on sandals—one of which had a hole in it—and walked with his mother to the small schoolhouse.

The daily school tradition was for boys and girls to form two lines and sing the school anthem. Peter got in line toward the back, ahead of a boy who was much bigger than him, and pretended to know the words to the anthem. For some unknown reason, the boy behind him shoved Peter forward. The momentum from Peter's fall knocked the boy in front of him down, who sent the one ahead of him down in a domino effect of falling boys. Peter got up, angry and embarrassed, and punched the boy in the face.

The furious teacher marched Peter to the principal's office, where the wall was decorated with punishment sticks: bamboo canes of different thicknesses. She chose one, told Peter to hold his hands out, and began beating his hands with the cane. He cried and ran home.

When Kiu saw Peter back home, his face wet with tears, and heard his story, she marched him back to the schoolhouse and right into the principal's office.

"You punished my son," she said.

"Yes." The principal leaned back in her chair.

"But you didn't punish the boy that pushed him?"

"We didn't see the boy that pushed him."

What she said next, Peter remembers so clearly because it surprised him. Kiu leaned in toward the principal's face, forcing her to lean slightly away. "Then my son will never go to this school again."

When Kiu and Peter left, he had mixed feelings. He wanted to go to school, but he didn't want to be slapped with sticks. On the other hand, if he didn't go to school, he could enjoy the freedom of a house empty of sisters all day.

What Peter didn't know about his mother's statement, and wouldn't until much later, was that Kiu meant Peter would never go to *that* school again. She had a plan. Chow, Peter's grandfather, had been saving up and now had enough money for the Chin family to fly to New York City to live with them in their apartment on East Broadway. All Kiu had to do was get approval through immigration and they could all go to America. Where there was work and food. Where school principals didn't beat children's hands.

It couldn't take long to get this paperwork approved, a few weeks at the most. It was fine for Peter to miss a little school. They would all go to the better place, where the streets were

paved and cars drove on them and the crops were not fertil-
ized from the stuff taken from the bathroom buckets.

Soon they would leave for a new school. A better school. A
better life . . . in America.

It took *two years* to get the immigration papers approved.

During that waiting period, Peter turned seven, then eight,
and spent his days helping his mother. Occasionally, they
would visit her sister in the city of Kowloon, where Peter saw
actual cars and roads and big buildings and people coming
and going. Then they went home to the dirt roads and the
small farms where cows were the only traffic.

In the New Territory of Hong Kong in the early 1960s,
everyone was poor. There were degrees of poor, and the richer
poor kids had these things called *toys*. These toys might consist
of a ball, a whistle, a bamboo flute, or a sword. The cheapest of
these toys, which meant they were the most prevalent ones,
were the paper kites. Almost every poor kid owned a paper
kite. Every poor kid but Peter.

Peter watched the kids with their kites and how they made the
colorful shapes roll in the wind as they rose and dove. He vowed
to himself, "Someday, I'll have the biggest kite in the sky."

Someday.

Many somedays passed.

In 1967, immigration finally approved the Chin family papers. They were going to America. The family packed up their
few belongings and headed to the airport.

When Peter got close to the airplane they would be taking at
the Pan Am terminal, he was amazed. He had seen big things
in Hong Kong but nothing like this. It was long and blue and
had wings, not like a bird's wings but, well—he didn't know
what it was like. He couldn't stop staring. Then he saw people
coming out of the plane.

Kiu pointed to the plane. "We're going in that."

Peter had no words. How could something so big take them
anywhere up in the sky?

When they entered the airplane, the wonder continued. The seats were soft and clean, and even the air smelled good. It had multiple bathrooms—*there was a bathroom in the airplane*—and *water* came out of the faucet. Back at your seat, uniformed ladies brought you food and drinks, and you didn't have to do anything for them. They just brought it to you. You could sit in that soft chair with your belly full and look down on the clouds. Clouds that were higher than even a kite could go.

The flight had a transfer in Hawaii and, while deplaning, Peter and his family were greeted by natives who put leis around their necks. The flowers smelled sweet and were beautiful and, even better, they were free . . . just like the Chin family now was. They all boarded another plane and once again soared above the clouds.

Six hours later, the Pan Am plane landed at Kennedy Airport in New York City. Peter stared out the window, transfixed, as the airplane got closer to the large cluster of buildings, landed, then rolled down the tarmac.

When it stopped, Peter turned to his sister Nancy. "Are we there?"

Nancy was already out of her seat, focusing on their mother's directions. They followed Kiu toward the door like baby ducks. The family of Chins, one adult and five children all under the age of twelve, walked out of the aircraft and onto US soil.

It must have been a drastic contrast for Kiu Chin to go from the quiet poverty of the New Territory outside of Hong Kong to the bustle and noise of Kennedy Airport in New York City. If she felt any disorientation, she didn't show it, or more likely didn't have time for it. She needed to get these children through a busy airport with signs and directions in a language she didn't understand.

Kiu blazed a trail through the waves of people, constantly making sure all her ducks were accounted for, until they reached the cab stand. Kiu worked her way down the line of cabs, asking each driver one simple question in Cantonese until she found one who didn't look confused but actually answered back. They all piled into that cab.

From the taxi, through Queens and Brooklyn, the family soon arrived at 92 East Broadway. They all poured out of the cab, unloaded their bags, and stood there on the street—from the quiet outskirts of Hong Kong to the noise of New York City in the very same day.

Peter heard the rumble of the trains above him on the Manhattan Bridge and stared at the six stories of the building that would now be their home, the tallest building he had ever seen this close.

An eight-year-old boy's monumental memories remain sharp and bright. Peter remembers walking into his grandparents' long apartment that ran from the front windows overlooking East Broadway to the back windows looking down on Division Street. He also remembers seeing the face of his grandfather, Chow Kong Chin, for the first time. The man who had saved them. The man who had faithfully sent them money to keep them alive. Peter looked at him, and both he and the old man smiled. Peter thought, *This is a nice man.*

The small apartment was alive now with the addition of the six new Chins. Bags were dropped, greetings were made, and soon the Chin children were exploring.

Peter walked into the one bedroom in the apartment and pointed to something he had never seen. Bunk beds filled the room. "What's this?" He touched one of the beds, pressing down on the spongy mattress.

"I think it's a bed." Victoria only guessed at this, since none of them had actually seen a real bed before. Not one with a box spring and a mattress. They giggled and sat on it and were soon jumping on the bed, laughing and jumping, higher and higher. Until—

Curses filled the room, booming shouts of a man Peter first thought was his grandfather, but no, this was a man they hadn't seen before. Some of the curse words Peter knew, but most he didn't. Peter and his sister slipped off the bed and out of the room. Whoever this new man was, he was not like Peter's grandfather. *This is a mean man.*

That first night in America, the entire family went out to a restaurant in Chinatown, the first restaurant the Chin children had ever been to. They all sat at a great round table where food was placed in large bowls before them. More food than Peter and his sisters had ever seen at one time—a great feast. Peter ate to his stomach's delight until his mother leaned over to him.

"Do you see that man?" she asked.

"What man?"

"There, on the other side of the table." She pointed.

Peter nodded and reached for more dumplings.

"That man is your father."

Peter didn't want to tell his mother that he didn't know what that word *father* meant, or that the man his mother pointed to was the mean man who had cursed at him and Victoria for jumping on the bed. Peter knew that whatever *father* meant, it was something you should probably avoid.

With the arrival of the five Chin children, Kiu, and this new person called *father*, nine people occupied the small one-bedroom apartment on East Broadway in New York. By the time Peter's sister Susan was born a few years later, the grandparents had moved to their own apartment, taking the population down to eight. Still, it was tight quarters, but the apartment was warm and dry, had real beds, a kitchen, and one amenity that few New York Chinatown apartments had: its very own bathroom. Most apartment dwellers had to share a communal bathroom.

A nice woman who lived on the sixth floor of their building who spoke both Cantonese and English was kind enough to help Kiu fill out the school enrollment paperwork. She knew that the Chin children would need American names, so she assigned each child their new name, one Americans could pronounce and write. Chin Chit Chuey became Peter Chin.

Within weeks of arriving in the United States, Kiu Chin, who kept her Chinese name, got a job at the clothing factory on Mulberry Street in Little Italy. This was great news because there was an understanding that Peter's father, Bark, would not financially contribute to the family. Ever. The reason was never made clear to Peter, but Bark's money was to be his own for food, drink, and gambling. Anything the family required had to be provided by Kiu. Her new factory job was much needed.

As the children began to settle into their new American life, they realized one important fact early on: their father, Bark, known within the tongs as the Cow, was a violent man. Unlike most violent men, Bark didn't need a reason to be cruel, such as a spilled drink, an unmade bed, or a disobedient child. He just was. They came to understand that if Bark was around, brutality would be there, too.

Peter always bore the brunt of Bark's violence. If Bark was in the apartment at the same time as Peter, the belt inevitably came out.

The only satisfaction, the only sense of control that Peter took from his father's violence, was that no matter how severe these beatings were and how often they came, Peter never cried. Not once in the five years he lived with his father did Peter cry when beaten.

For the first few years, these incidents happened only once a week. Peter's father worked as a chef at various restaurants out of town and in New Jersey, so he was only home one day a week. Later on, Bark took a job right in Chinatown, which meant he was home every day.

When Peter was eleven, he had the chance to go away for an entire summer. His older sister Maria had married and had a small laundry with her husband that had a few livable rooms in the back. If Peter helped them for the summer, he could stay with them. He loved this and got his first glimpse of the difference between the poor of Chinatown and the rich of other parts of Manhattan.

Peter knew that on Kiu's one day off a week, she loaded all the family's laundry into a wheeled basket and spent the day at the laundromat. Rich people sent their laundry out, while poor people wheeled it down the streets to laundromats.

While out on the laundry-delivering run, Peter took in all the wealth of New York. He saw the tall buildings, the doormen, the well-dressed people coming and going, and he also saw—*wow*—the limousines. Long black machines with a uniformed driver to take passengers anywhere they wanted. Rich people not only wanted fancy cars but also needed someone to drive them.

Peter Chin was amazed at these limousines and made another promise to himself: *One day, I will have one of these to drive me around.*

The summer went by and it was soon time for Peter to go back home . . . where his father was waiting for him. Where the beatings continued.

At the end of the year, Kiu had a nice surprise for her family. She had saved enough money to have their very first Chinese New Year celebration, the biggest holiday in Chinese culture. The girls cooked all day, and Peter reveled in the smells and sights of the specialized food and decorations.

Bark walked through the door and saw the festive table and his family hoped for a smile from him—or at least his approval. Instead, rage flared in his eyes and his anger erupted as he flipped the table over, kicking the dishes all over the apartment and smashing the food into the floor. Although Bark's violence didn't require a reason, something about that table and the family's hard-earned celebration triggered a desire in him to take it away. The same way that a toy given to the children had to be hidden from Bark, or he immediately destroyed it.

The family lowered their heads as they cleaned the mess and went to bed hungry. They never celebrated Chinese New Year again.

* * *

Kiu's factory job was a difficult one. The garments went from the large factory room filled with rows of women sitting at sewing machines to the pressing room—the only place men worked in the factory—and then on to Kiu at the end of the line. It was her job to put the items on hangers, attach price tags and any belt that was required, cover them in plastic, and get them out the door. Thousands of garments a day needed to go out the door. No excuses. It quickly became clear that the job was too much for one person to handle alone.

"If you can't handle it," her boss said, "there are plenty of women who can."

Peter's sisters began going to work with her to help. When he was old enough, around the age of ten, Peter began to help as well.

Part of Peter's job was to go and get the food for teatime, a tradition where a factory owner supplied a short break and refreshments for the factory's workers. It was Peter's job to go to the restaurant to get the tea and cakes, and he looked forward to it because this is when he saw *Uncle Tang*. Peter wasn't related to him but called him "Uncle Tang" out of respect.

"Hello, Uncle Tang." Peter smiled, walking into the restaurant.

"Well, it's little cow," Uncle Tang beamed, referring to Peter's father's nickname of the Cow.

As Uncle Tang got the order ready, he asked about Peter's mother and sisters and Peter never wanted to leave. The idea of an adult man who was not only kind but actually happy to see him was rare. Peter thanked Uncle Tang and took the food back to the factory.

Often, Peter and his mother worked all night, came home, and then Peter went to school. Sometimes he was so tired that he napped on a pile of garments in the factory before leaving.

One morning, as Peter and his mother headed to work

when there was no school that day, they passed a crowd on Mulberry Street.

"What's going on there?" Peter pointed to a man lying motionless on the sidewalk. The man wore a white shirt and had one arm crossed over his stomach.

Kiu looked at the man and the people milling around him.

"Oh, they are making a movie," she said, because that's what she believed.

It wasn't until years later that Peter learned this was actually the first dead body he'd ever seen, at the age of twelve. The dead man was Crazy Joe Gallo, the *caporegime* of the Colombo crime family. Gallo was killed outside a restaurant in Little Italy, right next to the factory door where Peter helped his mother.

A few years later, Peter and his mother were walking outside the apartment on East Broadway and saw another man shot on the street. Peter's mother didn't try to explain this one away as a film, only pointing to the dead man's hand. "His fist is clenched."

"So?"

"That means someone will avenge his death."

A few years after that, in the nightclub they were now walking past, Peter would watch this man's brother being killed right in front of him.

The irony of the New York school system was its mandate that all children attend regardless of their grasp of English while offering no resources for children who didn't speak the language. Those kids sat at their desks and listened to lessons spoken in words they didn't understand. Peter attended school starting at the age of eight without any previous education and moved up every year, even though he and many like him never learned to read, understand, or write English.

Nevertheless, he liked school and felt honored to be able to attend. The worst part was the members of two large Chinatown gangs, the Black Eagles and the White Eagles, who were always waiting outside when school let out. They focused on the Chinese kids, trying to recruit them. Because Peter was a poor Chinese kid who didn't speak English, he became a prime target.

"You need to quit this school shit and stop being a punk," they said.

Peter wanted to help his mother and to go to school, not to be a gangster. He had heard that word from his sister Victoria. She was talking to a boy on the street, and Peter remembered him because he was different from any Chinese boy he'd ever seen. He was sitting on the bumper of a car with his feet up on a hydrant, lounging. He wasn't hurrying somewhere, and his gaze wasn't lowered to the ground. He looked well fed and had long hair. A Chinese man with long hair who didn't have a job or obligations, who clearly did his own thing, was something different.

"Who was that?" Peter asked Victoria.

"Sparerib."

"Sparerib? That's a funny name. Who's he?"

"He's a gangster," she whispered in his ear, and although she spoke in Cantonese, she used the English word, *gangster.*

Gangster.

Peter didn't fully understand what that word meant, but like the word *father*, he felt it was probably something he should avoid.

It seemed to Peter that the world had its good guys, like his grandfather, the working dads of Chinatown, the cowboys on TV. Then there were the bad guys, like the gangsters and the bank robbers in the movies.

And his father.

Later, Peter learned firsthand what these gangsters were capable of. When he was twelve, two teenaged gang members pulled him into an alley and made him turn his pockets out, only to reveal two measly quarters. Thinking that Peter was holding out on them, they gave him a severe beating. Bleeding and badly bruised, the only thing Peter could think about was how angry his father would be if he saw him, so he tried to sneak into the apartment. His mother saw him first.

Worried but not knowing how to speak the language needed to get Peter to a hospital, Kiu took Peter to a man in China-town who practiced Chinese medicine. This man told Kiu that the bruises and cuts, the black eye and the swollen lip, would heal.

"But these bumps," he pointed. "See these bumps on the top of his head? Oh, these are very serious and could cause brain damage later on."

Kiu was so frightened and paid the man whatever he asked for to cure these bumps. The man shaved off all of Peter's hair and applied a bad-smelling tar to the top. Now he was bat-tered, bleeding, tarred, *and* he smelled. They managed to hide him from Bark until his hair began growing back.

At thirteen, the world changed for Peter one night when he, two of his sisters, and his mother were coming home late from the factory. It was after ten, but the clothes at the factory had to ship out the next morning, so all the Chin children had stayed to help their mother that night. They were exhausted, and all they wanted was to eat, sleep, and get ready for school the next morning. As they reached their apartment door, a fu-rious Bark yanked it open.

"Why the fuck you guys go out and play?" he screamed.

Play? Peter thought, but thinking was all that was allowed. The family didn't respond to Bark, just lowered their eyes and walked into the apartment in silence as Bark raged. Kiu went to take her shower, the girls began making dinner, and Peter went into his room to take off his shoes. Bark followed. The belt did, too.

The beating that followed was as severe as the beatings ever were, but no tears escaped from Peter. Perhaps furious that he was still unable to get Peter to cry—or maybe it was simply bound to happen eventually—Bark walked to the kitchen, yanked the frying pan from Mary's hand, and slammed the pan hard against her head.

Peter heard the loud *bong* and his sister's scream of pain.

It was the first time Bark beat anyone in the house besides Peter.

In a film or a novel, the boy would attack his father to protect his sister, causing the man to back down. In reality, results like that rarely occur. Peter did not attack his father, but he did cross a very important line, taking a step that would have serious repercussions. He yelled and cursed at his father, as five years of built-up tears flowed out of him.

Bark's face went dark, then contorted in absolute rage. He grabbed a kitchen knife and lunged at his son. Peter was too fast and dashed out the door.

Bark followed him. "Come back here, you little shit!"

These words followed Peter down to the street, where Bark continued to scream, his rage peaking. "How you gonna survive out here without me, huh? *How?*"

When Peter was far enough away, he turned, raising his fists in the air, and shouted, "With these!"

Peter had a five-dollar bill in his pocket that his mother had given him for helping at the factory and nowhere to go. He only knew that he could never go back home.

No one stood up to the Cow and got away with it.

Peter was thirteen and wouldn't return to that apartment for another thirty years. He would also never see his father again.

CHAPTER 2
The Mayflower

Peter ran and ran and ran, then stopped.

Where am I running to? Should I go left or right?

He knew only a few places in the world: a small circle around the apartment building, which included the school and the factory where he helped his mother. He decided to go in the direction of the school, where there was a park nearby.

His first night living on the streets, Peter slept in Seward Park. A bum chased him from one bench to another, but when he finally found one, he still couldn't sleep because of the rats running underneath. When the sun came up, he knew that life would be different from now on.

He couldn't go back to school. He didn't even know where he was going to sleep, so how could he worry about school?

Peter went looking for a job.

He begged for every type of job there was in Chinatown: restaurants, laundries, department stores, factories. They all said he was too young. In fact, at the newspaper office where Peter asked about delivering the newspapers, they actually threw him out.

"These newspapers are heavier than you," they chided, carrying Peter by his collar to the street, telling him not to come back.

Peter thought about reaching out to his grandparents, but they were old. He didn't want to be a burden.

He tried to make the five dollars last as long as he could. Aside from buying his big-ticket items of a toothbrush and toothpaste, the only *luxury* items he felt he needed, he spent twenty-five cents on a loaf of Italian bread each morning and made it last all day. His favorite places to sleep were in the stairwells of high-rise buildings because the residents took the elevators for the most part. These landings between floors worked well, with a bonus: no rats.

Soon, the five dollars ran out, and his stomach growled with hunger. A boy he knew from school named Colgate spotted him on the street and saw how hungry Peter was.

"I can't just bring you in," Colgate said. "My parents will kill me. But if I tuck away a little from my plate, I can sneak down some food to you later."

Peter followed Colgate to his apartment building and waited in a nearby park, watching for a flashing bedroom light to signal that he was bringing down the food.

True to his word, the lights flashed, and Colgate brought a bowl of rice and vegetables. Peter was so moved that he lifted the bowl up, like a torch.

"It's not just the food," Peter said, trying to stop his tears. "It's your kindness. I'll never forget this, and someday I'll pay you back."

The days went on, and Peter found different places to sleep and a little food along the way. He also heard that the Black Eagles knew he was no longer in school, and they had determined that this could mean only one thing: Peter had joined a rival gang.

The Black Eagles cornered Peter's friend Alan to find out which gang Peter had joined. Alan didn't know, so they beat him. Badly.

A few weeks later, Peter's sister Nancy went looking for him and found him brushing his teeth with water spraying out of a fire hydrant. The sight of her little brother brushing his teeth that way stopped her cold, and she fought to keep the tears inside.

"I left home, too," Nancy said as she approached. She told Peter that she had gotten an apartment with David, her boyfriend, and that she had a job at a supermarket making $1.60 an hour while still going to school. David had a job in a garment factory. Peter could come live with her and David.

For three days, Peter was safe and dry and fed, living in his sister's apartment. He went nowhere, did nothing, and allowed his mind to catch up. He thought about his father. His mother. His friend who had been beaten for no reason other than that he knew Peter.

What were his options?

Nancy wanted Peter to go back to school and to stay with her and David, but she was only seventeen, working part-time *and* going to high school. Even buying Peter a pencil for school would be a burden on her, much less food and anything else he needed.

Unbeknownst to Peter, this moment proved to be a pivotal point in the life of Peter Chin, where this single decision would determine the rest of his days.

Peter could stay with Nancy and David. It would be difficult. They would struggle. The three of them could try to find a way to survive together.

Alternatively, Peter could decide not to be a burden to his sister and find a different way to survive.

He made the second choice and set the path that would determine the next thirty years of his life.

Just like on TV, where there are good guys and bad guys in this world, Peter figured *if the good guys—including the businesses of Chinatown—don't want me, maybe the bad guys will. At least the bad guys have food. At least the bad guys have a place to stay. If I'm going to be a bad guy, I'll be the best one I can.*

In June of 1973, with resignation and a heavy heart, Peter left Nancy's apartment to seek out two people.

First, he found his friend who had been beaten. Alan's black eyes and split lip fueled Peter's anger.

"Do you want revenge?" Peter asked.

"Sure, but how?"

"I know someone."

Simply knowing *someone* gave him a sense of hope. He liked that.

They set off to find the second person they needed: Sparerib.

When Peter told Sparerib his plan, Sparerib grinned. At the time, Peter didn't know that Sparerib was a member of the Ghost Shadows, who were currently at war with both the Black Eagles and the White Eagles. Peter's plan benefited the Ghost Shadows.

Sparerib took them to an apartment, where he had a bag hidden. When he opened the bag, he asked Peter, "Have you ever fired a gun before?"

"I've never even *seen* a real gun before."

Sparerib placed the .22 revolver in Peter's hand. He gave a two-shot derringer to Alan. The boys left.

"Okay," Peter instructed Alan, a block from where the Black Eagles hung out. "As soon as we get to that light pole and see them, empty all your bullets."

Alan nodded, his expression tight. "Okay."

"Just start shooting."

"I will, I will."

Peter and Alan crossed the street, but some of the Black Eagles had spotted them and crossed to the other side to take cover behind cars. The element of surprise was gone, so Peter started firing. The Eagles fired back.

"Empty all your bullets!" Peter shouted.

"I am!" Alan yelled back.

Within minutes, Peter's gun was empty, and the Black Eagles

had retreated. Not a single bullet hit a person from either group, or even a car window. What *had* happened was that a line had now been crossed. Peter had attacked the Black Eagles, which meant that he was now their enemy.

When Peter took the derringer from Alan to give back to Sparerib, he opened up the gun. The two bullets were still inside. Alan hadn't fired at all.

Peter tilted his head, puzzled. "I was trying to save you. To help you."

Alan walked away. As Peter watched him go, he somehow knew that their paths would never cross again.

Peter returned the guns to Sparerib and relayed what had happened with the Black Eagles. Sparerib knew that Peter would now need Ghost Shadow protection.

Sparerib took Peter home with him, where he stayed in Sparerib's family's apartment for a week, until they could get him approved to move to one of the Ghost Shadow apartments on Avenue B and Second Street in Manhattan.

From that time on—from the age of thirteen until after Peter was first arrested at fifteen—he did not see his family. He wanted to distance them from the dangers of his new world. During lunchtime, Peter called the factory where his mother and sisters worked to check on them.

The Ghost Shadows quickly became his new family, and the new apartment soon felt like home. Peter was not yet a Ghost Shadow; he hadn't earned that right. Under their protection, he would live with them, learn from them, and survive with them.

Peter found himself surrounded by people with street names like Applehead, Mongo, Taiwanese Boy, and Stinky Bug. Since Peter was the youngest of the Ghost Shadows by six years, they dubbed him Kid Jai, the Kid. Anyone who saw this group together could easily determine who the Kid was.

Sparerib told Peter about how the Ghost Shadows got their name. How the group had once been called Qwon Ying.

The Qwon Ying existed before the Flying Dragons, even before the White Eagles or the Black Eagles. At one time in New York's Chinatown, there was only the Qwon Ying, a band of thieves who focused on quick robberies of stores and shops. These crimes became well known for their speed but also because this group was small and had no tong affiliation, adding mystery to who they were. This led a creative newspaper reporter to write an article that would change the identity of the Qwon Ying. In describing these crimes, the reporter ended the piece about them with *"They came in like a shadow and left without a trace . . . like a ghost shadow."*

These poetic words not only sparked mystery and fear throughout Chinatown but also impressed the Qwon Ying, who decided that this was a much better name. From that point on, the Qwon Ying became the Ghost Shadows.

Other gangs developed in Chinatown: the Flying Dragons, the White Eagles, and the Black Eagles. These groups began to stake out territory and branch out into the lucrative field of the extortion of Chinatown businesses. The Qwon Ying slowly got pushed back.

The Ghost Shadows had few members in those early days, two of whom were Timmy Lee, a.k.a. Giraffe, and Nei Wong. Wanting to elevate the gang from robberies to extortion, as the other gangs were doing, the Ghost Shadows approached a small vegetable store in Chinatown. They demanded $500 per month in protection money. However, the key to extortion, besides a great name, was having the muscle to back up the threat, which the Ghost Shadows didn't have. The store owner turned the Ghost Shadows over to the police.

Eight Ghost Shadows, including Giraffe, were arrested for extortion. Giraffe made bail but couldn't raise bail money for the rest of the Ghost Shadows, so Nei Wong, Giraffe, and seven other Ghost Shadows loaded a van with weapons and headed to Boston's Chinatown, a much smaller area. Their plan was to rob some On Leong gambling houses in order to fund the bailout for the remaining incarcerated members.

The Boston police must have received a tip of this potential crime because the Ghost Shadows' vehicle was quickly pulled over and all inside were arrested for possession of seven handguns, a high-powered rifle, and several hundred rounds of ammunition.

The Ghost Shadows were eventually released. In a twist, Nei Wong decided to stay in Boston and work for the On Leong Tong in one of their gambling houses. The On Leong had a $30,000 bounty on the Ghost Shadows, who had openly declared animosity toward the group, so it was curious how Nei Wong became connected to the On Leong and remained safe while there.

A few days later, Nei Wong reached out to Giraffe and told him that he had the money to bail out the other Ghost Shadows and to come to Boston to get it. Giraffe told no one and went to Boston.

Giraffe was walking along Beach Street in Boston's Chinatown when eight men surprised him, dragging him down a street to a lot behind a restaurant. They beat him and asked him who his conspirators were. Giraffe refused to answer. They beat him some more, but Giraffe would not give them names. They shot Giraffe four times.

With Giraffe out of the way, Nei Wong returned to New York, now as the Ghost Shadow's Dai Lo. This was the beginning of what is considered the second generation of the Ghost Shadows.

In the United States in 1973, life followed a basic path. People were born, grew up, and went to school until it was time to go to college or get a job. They earned money to provide for themselves and later for their own families. These people connected to their neighbors and their communities and followed the rules of town and state governments.

If there was a crisis, they called the police, the fire department, or various social or government agencies. If they needed a house or a car, they went to a bank and got a loan. If they didn't like their job, they found a new one. If they didn't get along with their neighbors, they moved to another neighborhood, or another part of the country. It was a life with options.

The structure was very different in Chinatown, New York, in 1973. For over a hundred years, Chinese and Asian immigrants had migrated to one concentrated part of New York.

As a result of outside animosity and even violence toward them, this community turned inward and learned not to trust that world beyond East Broadway, relying instead on the internal structure. Chinatown quickly became a self-contained, self-governing country of its own, where every necessity could be found within its walls—jobs, housing, infrastructure, government, financing, support—without ever needing to learn a different language or to connect to the world outside of Chinatown.

The population of Chinatown continued to grow throughout this period. According to census information, Chinese immigration to the United States jumped 85 percent from 1970 to 1980. In New York's Chinatown, Cantonese and Mandarin became the accepted written and spoken tongue, and English was virtually unnecessary.

This created a very tight community, one that was suspicious of the world outside but that also kept the residents dependent upon it. Someone who didn't like their factory job in Chinatown would find it difficult to accept a factory job in Charlotte or Austin, where they would encounter linguistic and cultural challenges. Their lives were contained to the ten-block radius of Chinatown.

The structure and power of Chinatown was unique. At the top of that structure and power were the tongs.

The tongs began as social organizations, places where recent Asian immigrants could go to get job training, to settle disputes, or to get loans. However, the tongs quickly became criminal organizations.

To understand Chinatown in 1973, one must understand the fact that every business, every shop, every store, every factory paid for protection. If a business did not want to pay for protection, a fire occurred, or a robbery, or a break-in, and this would continue until the owner began their monthly payments or sold the business to someone who would.

The threat of violence or some creative pressure often ensured payments. If there was a restaurant with ten tables in Chinatown that didn't want to pay, then ten gang members would show up, each taking a table and ordering just tea. They would stay there all day, drinking tea, reading the newspaper, preventing any paying customers from being seated.

This arrangement between gangs and tongs ensured that the gang received cash flow as well as certain benefits. If a gang's members were arrested, the tongs produced bail. If there was a business deal the gang wanted to get involved in, the tongs provided financing. If they needed weapons, housing, legal help, the tongs were there for them.

The other key element of Chinatown in 1973 was the great restaurants, produce, and stores. It also had gambling, and plenty of it.

Gambling was illegal in New York but because of the power and influence of the tongs, it flourished in Chinatown. In Boston, it wasn't uncommon to see police officers in uniform acting as paid security for these gambling houses. In New York, the police were a little more discreet.

At the time, Mott Street was the crown jewel of Chinatown and had been controlled for years by the Eagles. This group began as the White Eagles, but stayed in power for so many years that they eventually produced a younger faction called the Black Eagles, a subsidiary group. The White Eagles were the elder brothers, offering assistance when the younger Black Eagles required it.

In 1973 on Mott Street alone, there were eleven gambling houses. Each paid $10,000 a week in protection to the Black Eagles. The gang was therefore receiving $110,000 a week without needing to commit another crime.

At the top of the top of this power curve was Uncle Benny, who was the head of the most powerful tong, the Hip Sing. He was the Godfather of Chinatown.

Every gang had streets they controlled. Every gang was associated with a tong. Every gang but one. The Ghost Shadows. They operated on the fringes of Chinatown—the area no one really wanted—East Broadway and Essex Street.

If someone from a rival gang with a tong affiliation was arrested, they would be bailed out and be on the street the next day. If a Ghost Shadow was arrested, everything would stop and the Ghost Shadows would have to collaborate to commit a robbery to raise bail money. The same applied if they needed a lawyer, because there was no tong to help.

Because they didn't receive protection money or have illegal businesses and enterprises, all of their income came from crimes. Robberies, mostly. What was the most obvious target to rob in Chinatown? Gambling houses—protected by other gangs and sanctioned by a tong.

To combat the increase in robberies, the tongs offered a $35,000-a-head bounty to anyone who killed a Ghost Shadow. For perspective, the cost of an average two-family home in 1973 was $35,000.

Even before committing his first crime with the group, just by association, thirteen-year-old Peter Chin became a marked man with a $35,000 bounty on his head.

Each day, on the outskirts of Chinatown at the Wah Long Coffee Shop on 13 Chatham Square, the Ghost Shadows met with Nei Wong, the Dai Lo of the Ghost Shadows. When Peter turned fourteen, Nei Wong was exactly twice his age, twenty-eight.

"Don't talk to him," Mongo said to Peter that first time entering the coffee shop, nodding toward Nei Wong. "You're not part of the Ghost Shadows, and he is the Dai Lo."

As if Peter would have dared talk to the boss.

Peter tagged along, learned, checked in every day, and spent every moment with the Ghost Shadows. The days of going hungry were over because Ghost Shadows never paid for a meal in Chinatown. Ever. They all piled into a restaurant, ate their fill, then wrote the Chinese characters for Ghost Shadows on a piece of paper as payment. The waiters read it and bowed in acquiescence—not so much in fear of the Ghost Shadows but just in acceptance that they wouldn't pay the bill.

In Chinatown, gambling houses were everywhere, and people traveled from all over New York and beyond to gamble in them.

Since the Ghost Shadows were not associated with a tong, robbing any of the gambling house presented the risk of repercussions. The exception was the gambling house on Pell Street.

Pell Street was protected by Uncle Benny, the Godfather of Chinatown, and no one dared rob that one.

Shortly after turning fifteen, Peter was asked to participate in his first crime. The Ghost Shadows were going to rob the gambling house on the corner of Canal and Mott Streets. Most street gangs at that time were armed with .38 Special revolvers provided by the tongs. These were light and powerful weapons that could fire five rounds and quickly be reloaded.

However, because the Ghost Shadows weren't sanctioned, they used whatever they could get. These were mostly single-shot pistols. There was even one older gun that needed to be loaded with gunpowder and a ball. The Ghost Shadows called these weapons cowboy guns: bulky and unreliable handguns that, if fired, would require the shooter to retreat to a safe place to reload.

Sparerib placed the heavy gun in Peter's hand. "Make sure you don't need to fire twice."

A getaway car was parked halfway up on Mulberry Street—the only car the Ghost Shadows owned—and the six men left it, working their way through the waves of people toward the corner at Canal. When they arrived at the gambling house, the Ghost Shadows walked up two flights of stairs, pistols drawn, and stepped inside.

"Hands up!" Sparerib shouted.

The entire gambling hall stopped and stared at the men, then at the guns. The advantage of cowboy guns was that they're big and intimidating, especially if pointed at you. The people in the gambling house didn't move.

The majority of Ghost Shadows ran from table to table grabbing cash and stuffing it into bags, leaving Mongo and Peter to head to the side room where the safe was. A thin man with a mustache tried to block them, but Mongo charged right past him.

"Open it!" Mongo ordered, pointing the cowboy gun toward the man.

The mustache man responded, "I can't. I don't have the combination."

Mongo was about to beat the man with the butt of the gun when Peter stopped him.

"Let's take it with us."

"The safe?"

Peter knew this was a crazy idea, but he laid a thick blanket on the floor and pushed the safe onto it. Then he grabbed the end of the blanket and started pulling the safe, which slid across the floor. Mongo followed.

When the other Ghost Shadows saw Peter pulling the safe across the floor, they took this as their cue to follow, moving from the individual tables toward the door, helping to pull the safe. Despite their doubts, once outside, they pushed the safe down the two flights to street level, then began pulling the safe down the crowded street toward the car. As comedic as this sounds, it was then that Peter heard a voice yell "Stop!"

Peter turned and saw a horse-mounted policeman half a block up looking at them. Peter ignored him, and they all pulled the safe faster along the street.

Pulling a safe on a blanket through the busy afternoon traffic of Canal and Mott was difficult, but getting a large horse through that crowd was impossible. The Ghost Shadows pulled and yanked the safe forward as the policeman yelled for them to stop, powerless to pursue them.

Soon, they reached the car that was parked on Mulberry Street. They dumped the safe in the trunk along with the tattered blanket and thought about driving away, but the traffic made that risky, so they took off on foot. The officer was still blocks behind them and hadn't seen them stow the safe in the car.

Later that afternoon, the Ghost Shadows crept back to the car and drove to the apartment on Avenue B and Second Street, where they pushed and lifted the safe up to the second-floor apartment. They stayed for the rest of the afternoon, taking turns banging on the safe with a sledgehammer until it finally opened. The day's haul was over $100,000, more money than Peter had ever seen. It would fill the Ghost Shadows coffers, but not for long.

One day, when walking into the Wah Long Coffee Shop to check in, Peter saw that Mongo was already there, yelling at a man Peter didn't recognize. Peter ran to stand behind Mongo, trying to look as intimidating as a fifteen-year-old can. Mongo grabbed the back of the man's collar and made him face their boss, Nei Wong.

"Do you see this man?" he asked. "He doesn't like to wait for anything, especially money."

With that, Mongo began violently beating him.

Peter jumped in to help, and they both punched and kicked the man, breaking his nose, jaw, and several ribs.

"I'll pay," the man cried out, but the blows continued. Mongo and Peter pushed and kicked the man across the coffee shop to the bathroom, where they forced him into a stall and shoved his head in the toilet. The man stood up, looking at them both until Mongo motioned that the man could leave. Humiliated and bleeding, the man slunk out of the coffee shop with the promise to pay Nei Wong.

What Peter wouldn't know for another few months was that this man would change the course of Ghost Shadows history, as well as the history of Chinatown.

The man Mongo and Peter had beaten was Kai Hong Mak, a former Hong Kong policeman now living in Chinatown. The next and last time Peter would see him was at the Mayflower nightclub the night he would kill Nei Wong and be the first person to point a gun in Peter's face.

Peter was on the street corner when he heard the voice behind him. He turned as the first punch hit. His nose cracked, exploding with blood, the pain arriving seconds later as his vision crowded with stars. Peter lifted his hands to defend himself, ignoring the bleeding nose, and saw that he was surrounded by eight or so Eagles. He recognized an Eagle named Jackson, who was standing closest to Peter.

The Ghost Shadows had a small apartment on Avenue B and Second Street, big enough to hold several mattresses for everyone and cheap enough for them to afford the $150-a-month rent. It was cheap because it was one of the worst neighborhoods in all of New York and no one wanted to live there—right in the middle of no-man's-land, territory that no gang owned, so anyone had a right to be there.

"We know who you are." Jackson pushed Peter.

"Yeah, and we're going to fuck you up," another one said.

The next punch hit Peter on the side of the head, sending him spinning around and pushing him over a fire hydrant.

Blood poured out of his nose and he wiped it away. That was when Peter saw something on the sidewalk near the hydrant. An empty beer bottle. He grabbed it by the neck.

In the movies, when the character takes a beer bottle and smashes the end against something hard, it becomes a perfectly shaped shank of glass. This ruthless makeshift weapon not only is created in a dramatic fashion but gives attackers concern about continuing to assault their victim.

In reality, when Peter smashed the edge of the bottle against the hydrant, the bottle exploded in his hand, leaving him holding only the very end—way too small to be used as a weapon. Peter didn't let this stop him.

With blood pouring from his face and holding a tiny fraction of the glass bottle, Peter faced the group. "C'mon, you motherfuckers!"

Jackson looked at Peter, at his lack of weapons, and at the rest of the group. They decided that this skinny Ghost Shadow was far too unstable to deal with. They walked away.

Peter watched them leave. He dropped the tiny fragment of glass and walked back to the apartment to clean up.

The Ghost Shadows could be found in three major places on the days they were operating on the outskirts of Chinatown. One was the Wah Long Coffee Shop, the second was the car service on Henry Street, and the third was the Ghost Shadow base camps.

The car service on Henry Street was like a community center, a public hub of all things going in and out of Chinatown. People dropped off and picked up their cars at the service, and they also met and socialized there.

Clifford Wong was a waiter when Peter first met him at the car service. Clifford would later become the leader of the Tong On Association.

Another regular was a man named Paul Tang, who went by

the street name Dice. He was older than Peter by almost ten years and was married but would stop to talk to the Ghost Shadows and Peter. Dice had just gotten out of prison on a gun charge and always had one idea or another about a score he planned to make.

"Got a big one cooking." Dice would smile at Peter, pointing at his head. "This one could be huge."

Sometimes Peter would hear the idea, but more often than not, the idea would change into something different by the next time he saw Dice.

Dice was the rare breed of floater. He had no fixed loyalties but was cordially acquainted with countless people. It wasn't unusual for him to drink beer with the Ghost Shadows, play mahjong with the Flying Dragons, and eat with the Eagles.

The third place the Ghost Shadows frequented was the Mayflower nightclub, which happened to be across the street from Peter's family's apartment. The official name for the club was the Fai Do, which translates to Flower City, but the newspapers often referred to it as the Mayflower.

On the night of April 20, 1974, eight Ghost Shadows entered the Mayflower and took over a table. At a nearby table sat Nei Wong with a woman named Debbie. When the Ghost Shadows decided to go to a nearby gambling house to play Pai-gow (dominoes), Peter stood to go with them.

"No," said Sparerib. "You're too young to be inside a gambling house. Stay here."

Peter thought this was a little funny—he was old enough to help *rob a gambling house*, but he couldn't *go in one?* Peter said nothing, and Sparerib instructed Peter to hand his pistol off until they got back. Peter obeyed but had a bad feeling. For the last two years, it had been his constant companion.

Peter sat alone, waiting for the other Ghost Shadows to return, when a man entered the club and walked directly to Nei Wong's table. Upon reflection, Peter realized that the man had been tipped off about who would be sitting at that table, as he knew exactly where to go in the dark club.

Time tends to slow down at pivotal moments in life, and this happened for Peter. As the figure approached, Peter recognized him as the man he and Mongo had beaten up in the bathroom of the coffee shop: Kai Hong Mak.

Mak pulled out his gun and began firing.

Peter instinctively reached for his pistol, but it wasn't there. He ducked as bullets hit walls, glasses, mirrors, and, more horrifyingly, flesh with a *whump*. More shots pounded as both Nei Wong and Debbie fell to the floor. The club was filled with the screams and panic of customers running for cover, and Peter, only two feet away, watched the shooter turn to point the gun at him.

Mak gave a small smile of recognition to Peter. "I'm not going to shoot you."

Mak yelled for the lights to be turned on and for the police to be called. He sat calmly at the bar and waited to be taken away. Mak had killed the man he came to kill and was prepared to be arrested.

While Mak waited for the police, Peter walked over to where Nei Wong and Debbie lay dead. For no real reason that he can think of, Peter remembers counting the bullet holes. Nine. When the ambulance arrived, he saw that Debbie's and Nei Wong's lips had turned purple. They were the third and fourth dead bodies Peter had seen. There would be more.

On Sunday, April 20, 1974, the *New York Daily News* and other papers began their coverage of the Ghost Shadow leader, Nei Wong, and his violent murder. They reported that Debbie, Nei Wong, and Mak were involved in a love triangle gone bad, but Peter knew this wasn't true.

Mak had lost face from the beating that Peter and Mongo had given him. A beating approved by Nei Wong. Losing face was a painful experience that needed correcting.

When Peter walked with his mother all those years ago, he had seen Nei Wong's brother, Monkey King, dead on the street, with the clenched fist, in front of that very nightclub. Whether Monkey King had been avenged, as his mother had thought he would be, Peter didn't know. But vengeance had been served to his brother, Nei Wong.

The Ghost Shadows were now without a Dai Lo.

CHAPTER 3
Rising to the Top

Growing up in Hong Kong and New York's Chinatown, Peter knew the stories of ancient China, when the emperors were so powerful and cruel that groups would often rise up against them. These groups were frequently defeated, and when they were, to make sure that they didn't rise again, the emperor would kill nine generations of each offender's family. Nine generations of parents and grandparents, aunts, and uncles, were all killed, often in front of the rebelling group, who were forced to watch their entire families wiped out, one by one, before they themselves were killed.

These ancient people continued to rebel by creating secret societies and ways to identify themselves with elaborate hand signals, vowing to keep their groups and activities secret. This was the beginning of the modern-day Triads.

An awareness of this history may be one of the reasons Peter Chin took the precautions he did when joining his own secret Triad-influenced society. Peter wanted to protect his family against the Ghost Shadows' enemies, so he created distance between himself and them.

Over the next few years, Peter didn't see his sisters at all, saw his mother only once, and had no desire to ever see his father again. He did talk to his mother on the phone often. The

Chins had a phone in their apartment, but Peter didn't want to chance his father answering or earn his mother or sister a beating just because Peter had called, so he called the factory where his mother worked. If he called during her lunch break, he knew his mother would be near the phone and could talk.

One day when Peter called his mother at work, his sister Mary—who also worked at the factory—picked up. Mary was crying.

"What's wrong?" Peter asked.

"He broke her arm," Mary cried. "That bastard broke her arm."

Peter didn't have to ask who *that bastard* was. He knew. His father, in one of his fits of rage, had broken his mother's arm.

Slamming the phone down, Peter checked his pistol. It was loaded. He stuck it in the back of his belt and headed out.

A fire burned in Peter Chin. He was filled with anger but managed to keep it cool while he checked the coffee shops and the gambling houses that his father frequented. *The leg,* Peter thought. *I'll look him in the eye and then shoot him in the leg. Let him writhe around the street for a while until an ambulance comes to get him.*

Peter went to coffee shop after coffee shop, gambling house after gambling house, but the Cow was nowhere to be found. Peter was about to start over and begin checking them all again when two police officers approached him.

"Hold it!" they yelled. "Hands in the air!"

Peter obeyed. When one officer patted him down, he found Peter's pistol.

"We call this 'hunting,'" the other officer said to Peter. "That's what it looked like you were doing, looking for someone, which is why we stopped you. So, who you looking for, kid?"

Peter didn't answer. The officers brought him in and booked him on a weapons charge. He was sentenced as a juvenile and sent to the Bronx Detention Center for three months. It was his first arrest.

Every night in the juvenile hall, Peter and the other inmates were given their reward for the day: two small half-pints of milk, four cookies, and two Kool brand cigarettes. Peter thought it was funny that in New York in 1974 the legal age to buy cigarettes was eighteen, which meant that the state was breaking its own law each night.

If the Ghost Shadows hadn't forced restaurants to take their signature as payment, and if they hadn't managed to rob a gambling house, they would have gone hungry. There was no other income stream. Their weapons were old and unreliable. They stayed in a series of apartments they could barely afford. They lived a hand-to-mouth existence.

On top of that, they had a huge bounty on their heads that left them constantly looking over their shoulders. This created the unexpected advantage of complete loyalty within the Ghost Shadows, relying on one another for absolutely everything. That unity created great strength. Desperation mixed with strength is a powerful combination.

In 1974, the Ghost Shadows were a criminal organization operating on the outskirts of Chinatown. Few had heard of them, and even fewer feared them. With the loss of their leader, the gang found themselves at their weakest point. It was at this time that fifteen-year-old Peter Chin was released from juvenile hall and officially became the gang's youngest member.

In Italian organized crime there is a ritual called being *made*: a clearly defined ceremony involving the photo of a saint, a drop of blood, and a pledge of lifelong allegiance to that criminal organization. The Chinese Mob had variations of this ceremony, mostly stemming from Triad rituals of long ago. Some of these were elaborate, involving drinking snake or pig blood, sometimes mixed with wine. This was Peter's experience.

In a small apartment, Sparerib, the Ghost Shadow who had brought Peter in, stood with him and two other Ghost Shadow members. Peter was positioned in front of a statue of General Kwon.

If you've ever been to a Chinese restaurant, you've probably seen a small statue of Buddha, or a statue of General Kwon. General Kwon will likely be facing a door with his battle axe up, ready to fight, and he will be wearing red shoes. Red is the color of protection, and General Kwon is there to protect the restaurant and those who go there.

There is a second General Kwon. This one has black shoes, which is the color of power, and his battle axe is pointed downward. This general isn't ready to fight; he has already made a kill. This is the gangster's General Kwon.

With candles and incense burning, Peter faced the gangster's General Kwon. As others read the lines, Peter repeated them to the general.

"If you betray your brothers, God will punish you."

"If I betray my brothers, God will punish me."

Peter needed to stay even farther from his family now. To protect them.

"If you betray the Ghost Shadows, God will punish you."

"If I betray the Ghost Shadows, God will punish me."

He had to keep his mother and sisters safe. Safe meant distance.

"If you think of yourself before your brothers, God will punish you."

"If I think of myself before my brothers, God will punish me."

This was his family now.

It was official. Peter Chin was a Ghost Shadow.

As Peter was beginning to feel part of this new family, news came from his sisters. Peter's mother had placed her hand over the open flame of the stove. She said she did this *to feel something, to feel anything.*

The years of physical and psychological abuse by Peter's father had finally caused Kiu to have a complete mental breakdown. She spent the next three years in a psychiatric hospital.

After midnight on December 3, 1974, Peter and eight other Ghost Shadows walked into the Jade Chalet restaurant at 199

Worth Street in Manhattan. The bar was one of their regular stops within the borders of the no-man's-land of Chinatown, and it was relatively safe.

When they opened the door, the cold of the damp street mixed with the familiar heat and smoke of the bar. What they weren't expecting was the *noise.*

"Holy fuck!" Mongo exclaimed as they walked in, initially believing there must be an unusually large crowd at the Jade Chalet. Then they saw that the crowd was normal size and the booming sounds were coming from one place. From just one table. From just two men.

These two men, Joe Heineman and Lou Cupo, sat at a table by the wall. They were very drunk, and they were very loud.

"Jesus," Mongo muttered as he took his seat, the rest following. They ordered drinks and tried to talk, but the noise from that one table was overpowering.

"Want to go somewhere else?" Applehead asked.

"Fuck that." Mongo turned in his chair toward the table.

"Hey!" he called out, but the two men ignored him.

"*Hey!*" Mongo yelled louder. This time he gained their attention. "Shut the fuck up!"

"Fuck you," Cupo shouted back.

Heineman grabbed an empty glass from the table and threw it at the Ghost Shadows. The glass shattered. As it did, Cupo began throwing more glasses and empty bottles at the Ghost Shadows.

This resulted in Heineman reaching behind his back to pull out his pistol. Peter saw this and grabbed for his pistol but couldn't get it out before Cupo fired. Then Heineman fired, and the Ghost Shadows returned fire. Within minutes, the small bar was an explosion of gunfire.

When the shooting was over, bar patron Jimmy Leong was on the floor, holding the gunshot wound on his leg. Tsu Wu, who had come into the bar for a beer after work, was dead.

When the police arrived, Heinman and Cupo—who were

actually off-duty plainclothes police officers—gave their version of the night to the officers first on the scene. The Ghost Shadows were all arrested and sent to Rikers Island to await trial. Peter, still a minor, was sent to the juvenile detention center in the Bronx for the second time.

Back to the world of milk, cookies, and cigarettes.

For three months, the Ghost Shadows were incarcerated while the state prepared its case against the gang. However, when police internal affairs got involved, several details of the case were questioned.

The two officers claimed that they'd seen the group of Ghost Shadows walk into the bar and decided to follow them. However, responding officers on the scene admitted that the two men were highly intoxicated and had obviously been drinking for some time. If so, they had been drinking while carrying their sidearms, a clear violation of protocol. The biggest concern was the ballistics reports proving that the bullets that wounded Jimmy Leong and killed Tsu Wu came from a police-issued 38, not from the .22-caliber handguns the Ghost Shadows carried.

The state decided to drop the case against the Ghost Shadows and to discipline the two officers internally.

The Ghost Shadows were all released from custody.

In a twist of fate, a similar incident occurred just a few months later when the Ghost Shadows walked into the Sun Tong Gung restaurant on Pell Street. Two officers were sitting at a table eating. Some of the Ghost Shadows recognized and began taunting them. The taunting was returned. Soon, the restaurant was like a scene from a Western movie, with tables tipped over and guns firing from both sides.

The Ghost Shadows were arrested again. Peter tried to lie about his birthday since he had just turned sixteen, which meant that he was no longer a minor in the New York penal system. He was sent to juvenile detention until they checked his birth date. Once they did, he was transferred to Rikers Island to await trial.

This time, no one was injured from the gunfire, so the police department dropped the case, wanting to avoid the backlash of yet another incident involving police gunfire in a place of business around civilians.

By the age of sixteen, Peter Chin had been arrested twice for shooting at the police. This was around the same time he lost his mentor to the justice system.

Sparerib had brought Peter into the Ghost Shadows, housed him, fed him, protected him, and taught him. Peter considered him a brother and a friend, but now he was going away for a while. Sparerib had been fighting an extortion charge that had gone to trial, and he received a guilty sentence—three years at Rikers Island.

The absence of Sparerib was felt by Peter and the Ghost Shadows, but they all quickly recovered when Yin Poy Louie, a.k.a. Nicky Louie, was released from prison.

Nicky Louie was a smart, driven, second-generation Ghost Shadow, following in the footsteps of his brother. He was handsome, with a rock-and-roll look that gave him the appearance of being much older than his nineteen years. After his release, Nicky Louie quickly reconnected with the Ghost Shadows, and they embraced him. Nicky saw the gap that had been left with the loss of Nei Wong's leadership and the absence of Sparerib's strength, so he took on those roles.

The Ghost Shadows accepted Nicky taking control. No one challenged his authority; in fact, they welcomed it and showed immediate loyalty to him. Nicky Louie was soon the new Dai Lo and became the leader the group needed.

Life moved on until one day Peter overheard Mongo talking nervously to Taiwan.

"What's wrong?" Peter asked.

"The Eagles," Mongo said. "They've kidnapped Nicky."

Peter was furious. "Well, let's get him back!" He pulled his .22 from the back of his belt loop. "They can't take our king!"

Peter let those words hang in the air for a while.

Our king.

Peter felt that Nicky was *their king*, and the Eagles couldn't have him.

Rallying behind Peter, the Ghost Shadows moved in formation down Chatham Street and then Pell Street, looking in every bar and café for any clue about what had happened to their leader.

Peter stood on the corner of Mott, crossing into Eagle territory, and saw some Eagles across the street, so he pulled out his pistol, firing one shot toward them. As in most cases when Peter fired a weapon, he missed. Completely. Peter was a terrible shot. To add to this particular farce, after shooting once, Peter's gun jammed.

Peter bent down to try to unjam the small gun when ten shots were fired back at him, blasting the stop sign behind, missing him by inches on all sides. The difference between the pop sound of Peter's .22 and the booming explosion of the .38 used by the Eagles was vast.

Peter ran to join the others, who were now moving at a high speed down Mott Street, ready to kick in door after door to get their king back.

"Wait," Mongo said, and halted. The group stopped running and followed Mongo back to where he pointed at a building. There, in a bar that he rarely went to, Nicky sat drinking with a Ghost Shadow member named Pork Chop. Mongo and the group walked in, bewildered.

"What's wrong?" Nicky asked.

"What's wrong?" Mongo repeated. "We heard you got kidnapped!"

"Kidnapped? I've been right here." The smile on Nicky's face told another story.

Peter never said anything, but he knew right then that this had been a test. Nicky wanted to see how loyal the Ghost Shadows would be to their new leader. To their new king. Peter figured they had all passed.

*   *   *

One of the first things Nicky Louie wanted to do was to change the territory of the Ghost Shadows because Chatham Square was no place to make a living or to make their mark. Nicky decided they needed to take Pell and Doyers Streets, which would mean stealing territory away from one of their enemies, the Flying Dragons. These were the least important streets under the Flying Dragons' control, but if the Ghost Shadows could establish themselves there, they could gain a hold into Chinatown.

When Nicky Louie told the Ghost Shadows that they were going to take territory from the Flying Dragons, there was no resistance.

"There are only twelve of us," they said loyally. "But we have thirteen guns."

They were referring to the shortest of the Ghost Shadows, a boy with the street name of Japanese, who always carried two pistols.

Twelve members were all they needed.

The Ghost Shadows planned how they would take territory from the Flying Dragons and from their leader, Michael Chen, known as the Scientist.

The fact that the Ghost Shadows—with no tong affiliation and no true income source—were the poorest of the poor, going against a larger tong-supported group, didn't matter to them. Desperation was their common fuel, and their poverty meant that they had nothing to lose.

To call the event when the Ghost Shadows took Flying Dragon territory on Pell and Doyers Streets *a battle* would be an exaggeration. In an unusual mix of luck and timing, when the Ghost Shadows arrived, the Flying Dragons—who should have been stationed at the street to protect it—weren't there. Part of this luck could have been due to the fact that the head of the Flying Dragons was in prison at the time, leaving the group somewhat disorganized and less disciplined.

The Ghost Shadows walked right in, crossing the border

into Flying Dragon territory on Pell. Finding it unguarded, they simply began to take it over. Not a shot was fired nor a beating administered.

When the Flying Dragons came back and saw that the Ghost Shadows had established a solid territory on Doyers and Pell, including soldiers on guard and a meeting place, the Flying Dragons didn't try to reclaim it. Instead, they moved that group to Queens.

Doyers and Pell Streets now belonged to the Ghost Shadows. Doyers and Pell were not only considered Chinatown proper but also housed businesses to extort, which meant that a small income could be made there.

This move established the Ghost Shadows as somewhat legitimate in the Chinatown organized crime hierarchy, while creating cash flow for the group. It also did one other important thing: it caught the attention of Uncle Benny, the Godfather of Chinatown, the head of the Hip Sing Tong.

Uncle Benny had been a fixture in Chinatown since the 1950s when he was released from prison and became the second in command of the Hip Sing under his brother, Sam Ong, known as Uncle Six. When Sam died, Uncle Benny stepped in and continued to build his strength, his wealth, and his reputation in Chinatown.

By 1976, Uncle Benny was at the height of his power and was often called the Mayor of Chinatown or the Principal of Pell Street. Despite all the power and wealth—including a reach that went from coast to coast, to the Triads of Hong Kong, and beyond—Uncle Benny rarely left Pell Street in New York.

Uncle Benny spent most of his time between his home there and the Hip Sing Tong on 15 Pell Street. He enjoyed walking around the neighborhood for exercise, always followed by at least one bodyguard.

Uncle Benny knew that the Ghost Shadows were becoming a group that would soon need to be brought into one of the tongs, and he wanted them to come to him instead of to the rival On Leong Tong.

This offer could have been a simple business move, a logical next step, except for one interesting fact: when the Ghost Shadows went to the Hip Sing to be initiated, Uncle Benny attended. Uncle Benny had not been part of any initiation ceremony in many years, but for reasons that are still unclear, he wanted to be a part of the Ghost Shadows becoming Hip Sing. He arrived at the Hip Sing office and climbed the three floors to the initiation room to participate.

On the day of the initiation, twelve Ghost Shadows arrived at the Hip Sing building on 15 Pell Street. Incense was burned, phrases were repeated in front of the gangster's General Kwon statue (black shoes, battle axe drawn down), and promises were made. When the ceremony was over, Uncle Benny welcomed each Ghost Shadow with a "red envelope"—a gift of cash.

Uncle Benny also gave the Ghost Shadows a basement apartment he owned on Doyers Street to use as their new base. The same basement used by Mock Duck, the infamous criminal leader of the Hip Sing Tong in the early 1900s.

In a matter of months, Nicky Louie had moved the Ghost Shadows farther than ever before. Now that the gang was on Pell Street, they saw more of Uncle Benny and visited him often.

Because Uncle Benny was getting older, he often didn't want to climb the three flights to the top floor where the initiations took place. He did most of his business in a large conference room on the main floor. While the Ghost Shadows talked to Uncle Benny in the conference room, Peter saw something in the corner that caught his eye: a bright red tricycle. Peter had no toys growing up and didn't really know what was involved in riding a tricycle, which was almost a bicycle, and he hadn't ridden one of those, either. He figured he could probably ride the tricycle since it had three wheels. *If* he could fit on it.

While the other Ghost Shadows talked to Uncle Benny

about upcoming extortion payments, Peter walked over to the tricycle and sized it up.

In the middle of the conversation with Nicky and Mongo, Uncle Benny heard a squeaking sound. He turned and saw Peter—his legs folded up and shoulders hunched over the way-too-small tricycle—peddling around the large conference room.

Uncle Benny scowled, ready to reprimand this young Ghost Shadow, but then he saw the smile on Peter's face.

"It's my grandson's," Uncle Benny informed him. "Don't break it."

Realizing he might have made a mistake, Peter got off the tricycle. At least now he had ridden one.

Life on Pell Street became good for the Ghost Shadows, so much so that they were comfortable without their weapons. If they traveled outside the territory to streets owned by the Flying Dragons or the Eagles, they brought pistols. On their own turf, they moved around unarmed.

One day while heading down Pell Street, the Ghost Shadows encountered a group of Eagles on the corner of Pell and Mott Streets. The Eagles saw them and without warning pulled out their guns and began firing. With no weapons, the Ghost Shadows ran to their location on Doyers Street to get their guns, passing right by Uncle Benny.

"What's going on?" Uncle Benny asked Peter.

"The Eagles," Peter said, panting, "are shooting at us. We're getting our guns."

Uncle Benny's face hardened. "Those sons of bitches," he said, taking Peter by the hand like a child and running *toward* the Eagles.

Peter let himself be pulled along by Uncle Benny, like a schoolkid being led toward a neighborhood bully by his mother, even though Peter knew they were heading toward the gunfire instead of away from it.

When they got to the corner, the Eagles had left.

Uncle Benny released Peter's hand.

"Sons of bitches," he repeated.

"You look like shit." Peter heard Nicky's voice, but it seemed far away. Nicky put his hand on Peter's forehead. "Holy fuck, you're burning up."

Peter stood in the doorway of—well, of somewhere. He looked around and tried to remember where. He was tired and clammy and quickly becoming aware that he didn't feel very well. There was more talking in the background, and he tried to listen, but it seemed so far away.

"What?" Peter asked.

"I said, let's go to my mother's apartment, Kid. You can rest there."

Nicky walked Peter to the apartment Nicky's mother lived in over a small grocery store they owned, ABC Grocery Store, at 67 Eldridge Street. He led Peter up to apartment 3 and showed him to a bed. Before leaving, he took Peter's temperature.

"Shit," Nicky frowned. "Temp's 103. Get some rest, Kid." Nicky left and Peter passed out.

Over the next several hours, Peter floated inside the restless sleep of the sick until he heard the voice again.

"Kid, we gotta go. We gotta do that thing."

Peter opened his eyes. It was dark now and it took him a moment to remember where he was. *Okay, I'm in Nicky's mother's apartment. Why? Oh, yeah, sick.*

Nicky scowled and felt Peter's forehead. "Holy shit, you're still burning up."

"Hey." Peter sat up in the bed. "You said we gotta go, so let's go."

Even in his feverish fog, Peter knew what *that thing* was. Every man was needed because *that thing* was big. This was verified when Nicky handed Peter the shotgun.

Peter looked at it. "I have my pistol."

"You'll need this, too."

The shotgun had both the barrel and the stock sawed off, so it was more of a pistol than a rifle, with holes drilled in the stock for a strap to go through. Peter placed the strap around his shoulder and put on the long trench coat that would hide the weapon. The two headed out into the cool November night.

They met up with the other Ghost Shadows, twelve total, and Nicky explained the plan again.

"We're taking over Mott," Nicky said. "No one has ever done this before."

"There's a reason why," a Ghost Shadow replied, and they laughed. It wasn't a fear-filled laugh but one of excitement. One of anticipation. One of finally doing something to change their state.

The plan was simple. The Ghost Shadows would team up and move in groups of two, heading down Mott from all sides, moving toward the center, blocking in the Eagles. There would also be two Ghost Shadows stationed on roofs with rifles. If possible, no one died on either side; this would create too much heat. If possible.

They headed out. Peter and Lefty got into position on Mott and Pell, the others came in from Canal, and at eight o'clock on the night of November 14, 1974, it began.

Understanding how quickly the Eagles responded to this Ghost Shadows' attack on Mott Street demonstrates how important borders were in Chinatown. If a gang owned a street and another gang needed to pass through it, they needed to ask permission to borrow that street. If they didn't have permission, the safest route was to travel through unarmed to show they didn't mean any violence. Peter remembered that as a kid, Canal Street was the clear border between Chinatown and Little Italy. If Peter or other Chinese kids crossed into Little Italy and were chased out, the Italian kids chased them only to Canal and did not across it. Street corners and cross streets were recognized borders, as if they had checkpoints and guards.

When the Eagles who were guarding Mott Street saw Ghost Shadows crossing onto Mott from all directions, armed, that could mean only one thing. Shouts sent up alarms down the streets, and before the Ghost Shadows' feet even hit the street, shots were fired. They fired back.

In the first wave, some Eagles escaped, running out past Mott Street, and the Ghost Shadows let them go. Others ran into the gambling houses for safety and the Ghost Shadows followed them in.

Mott Street is only one block from the Fifth Police Precinct. It didn't take long for the gunshots to draw the police in, sirens wailing. When they did, the Eagles and Ghost Shadows scattered, hiding weapons and pulling back. The police searched, found nothing, and left. Minutes after this, the fighting began again. The police came three times to Mott Street that night to investigate the shots but found nothing.

When the Ghost Shadows captured an Eagle, they dragged him to the street and beat him violently, then sent him away. This continued as the number of Eagles steadily went down. When the Ghost Shadows saw no additional Eagles, they searched each and every gambling house to make sure none were hiding.

By five the next morning, the Eagles were gone and the Ghost Shadows had taken over Mott Street.

Peter Chin participated with a 103-degree fever.

When the dust settled on the new ownership of Mott Street, the financial advantage to the Ghost Shadows became clear. Each of the eleven gambling houses on Mott Street paid $10,000 a week in protection, which went into the Ghost Shadows' treasury. Each gambling house also paid a salary to the gang. On top of the $10,000 a week, another $16,000 a week per gambling house went to individual members. Nicky, as Dai

Lo, received the biggest portion, $1,000 a week. The next biggest portion went to the five generals, the most trusted members of the Ghost Shadows and those who held the highest rank: Mongo, Taiwan, Applehead, Stinky Bug, and Kid Jai. Each of the five generals received $500 a week per gambling house. Each of the soldiers received $200 a week.

Peter Chin received a salary of $5,500 a week, from the gambling houses alone. At this time, the average American made $11,000 a year.

This money would come a little later. But to celebrate his new power and prosperity right then, Peter Chin did one thing he had been waiting to do. He had his father officially kicked out of the On Leong Tong, an act that caused his father to lose face and be disgraced. This disgrace didn't last long, as the Cow simply joined the Hip Sing Tong. Still, Peter felt a surge of power that he'd never had with his father.

Life was good for Peter as the Ghost Shadows settled in. One day, while on the street on guard duty, Peter saw three pretty girls walking down Mott Street. They were all pretty, indeed, but he couldn't take his eyes off the girl with the silkiest hair he had ever seen. Her name was Ida May Wong, and with Peter's newfound confidence, he approached her.

CHAPTER 4
The General Becomes the Leader . . . and Goes to War

When the Ghost Shadows took over Mott Street from the Eagles, it wasn't a battle in a war where the enemy simply attempted to take that territory back. The Ghost Shadows were growing rapidly, with a membership of over seventy men, making them one of the largest criminal organizations in New York. As a result, the Eagles couldn't just retake Mott Street, so they decided to kill as many Ghost Shadows as they could. Whenever they could.

The Ghost Shadows were hunted like never before.

On April 19, 1975, Peter stepped off the sidewalk and was heading to one of the hangout apartments when he passed by a young Ghost Shadow called Ah Fong.

"Where you going?" Peter asked.

Ah Fong smiled. "I'm going to see my girl."

Knowing that Ah Fong's girl lived outside Mott Street, Peter was concerned because the girl lived on the outskirts of Chinatown, which was now Eagles turf.

"Why don't you take one of the guys with you?"

"Oh, I'll be fine," Ah Fong reassured Peter.

Ah Fong walked the four blocks to a pay phone on Eldridge Street to call his girl and tell her he was on his way. A car full of Eagles spotted him, drove around the block, and shot him in the phone booth, killing him.

In 1975, the cost of ruling the key territory of Chinatown was high.

At the same time, another power shift was occurring in the Chinatown on the opposite coast. In San Francisco, the Wah Ching, a once powerful criminal organization, had split off into a second group called the Joe Boys. The Joe Boys grew so rapidly that they soon overtook the Wah Ching in numbers, territory, and power. These once-connected groups were now at war with each other.

Fighting as long as they could, ten or so of the Wah Ching decided to try life on the other coast and came to New York's Chinatown for a fresh start. Seeing no threat in this small group of vagabonds, Nicky Louie brought them in as a sort of subcontractor faction of the Ghost Shadows.

One member of the Wah Ching was a man named Danny Wong, who went by the street name Ah Pai. A little older than Peter, Danny was assigned with Peter to the night shift to watch over the gambling house on Canal Street. Danny and Peter became friends; in fact, they got an apartment together on Chrystie Street.

Every evening, Peter and Danny watched the individuals with pockets full of cash walk into the gambling house. "You know," Danny said one night, "we used to have it like this."

"Have what?" Peter asked, scanning up and down the street.

"All of this." Danny waved his hand over the crowd. "The Wah Ching. We used to have in San Francisco what you have here. The Joe Boys have it now."

Peter lit a cigarette. "Take it back."

Danny laughed. "You can't just take it back. There are so many of them now."

This time it was Peter's turn to laugh. "Do you know how many Eagles there were when we took this over? There were only twelve of us. You have to have heart."

"*Heart.*" Danny smiled.

Peter knew what Danny was thinking. Having heart was a naïve thought, and it couldn't beat guns.

Days went by, and this time Peter brought up the subject when they were guarding the gambling house on Canal Street.

"Let's take it back." Peter watched a man come out of a phone booth.

"Take what back?"

"San Francisco." The man turned a corner and Peter relaxed. "Let's take it back for the Wah Ching."

Danny laughed but let this sink in a bit before responding. "You serious?"

"Yeah." Peter tossed a cigarette to the sidewalk and ground it out with his shoe. "I just need to tell Nicky that I'll be gone for a few weeks, but then we can go."

That was it. Soon Peter was on a plane heading to San Francisco.

When he got to California, Peter met with Vincent Jew, a rising force in the Wah Ching. He thanked Peter for helping them.

In San Francisco, Peter was introduced to a few more of the Wah Ching and to a man named Terry, who handed Peter a .22 pistol.

Peter examined the tiny gun. "This is what you're giving me? What do your other guys have?"

"The same thing," Terry answered. "We all have them."

"And how many of you are there? How many Wah Ching with .22s are out here?"

Terry thought about this for a minute. He added up all the Wah Ching in prison—there were a lot—and those that had been killed, determining how many were left. "About six, I think," he said. "Maybe seven."

Peter allowed a few seconds to process this. The Joe Boys had at least three hundred guys on the streets of San Francisco's Chinatown. Three hundred against six? There was *heart*, and then there was *math*.

Terry, Terry's girlfriend, and Peter drove around San Francisco's Chinatown so Peter could see everything. In the same way that a cop can spot a cop, a street guy can spot another street guy—the way they dress, the way they carry themselves. The Joe Boys didn't wear colors or uniforms, but they didn't have to. Peter saw that the Joe Boys were all around them.

At eight o'clock on that first night, the battery on the old Camaro died. It was getting dark and with all the Joe Boys around, Peter felt like a sitting duck.

"Let's push it to that garage." Peter pointed to the garage on Jackson Street. When they did, they positioned the car between the sidewalk and the garage for cover. A black-topped white Monte Carlo filled with several Joe Boys cruised by.

Peter moved closer to Terry. "Do you know a white Monte Carlo with a black top?"

"No," Terry said. "I just got out of prison."

Peter watched the car turn the corner and knew right away that something was going down.

"Get out of the car," he said, jumping out from the back seat. "They're coming."

A second later, they heard the sound of Monte Carlo car doors opening and closing, and soon a group of Joe Boys turned the corner. They all wore the same kung fu jackets and had huge handguns swinging from each hand. The Wah Ching scattered, and Peter realized that he was now in the open, so he ran into the garage. The Joe Boys followed.

The only thing big enough to offer protection was the hydraulic shaft of the car lift. This wouldn't offer much protection to an average man, but for skinny sixteen-year-old Peter Chin, it worked well—but only if he stood directly in front of it.

Shots began ringing out as three Joe Boys entered the garage. One in the center shot at Peter, but Peter was directly in front of the hydraulic shaft. The man on the right fired, but Peter had moved to the left to protect himself, then to the right when the third tried to shoot; all this time Peter was trying to count the bullets that were firing.

If they have heart, Peter thought, *and they all move in at the same time, I'm dead.*

The Joe Boys either didn't have heart or ran out of bullets, because they soon retreated, leaving the sounds of a screaming woman in the back seat of the Camaro.

Terry's girlfriend hadn't gotten out of the car in time, so she had hidden behind the front seat. A bullet had hit her hand and shattered the bone. She was screaming in pain. The group got inside the car, now covered with bullet holes, and headed for the hospital.

The next day they were back, driving through Chinatown, with Terry driving and a Wah Ching named Teddy Bear sitting next to him. Peter and Danny sat in the back. As the car climbed one of San Francisco's many hills, Peter happened to look in the rearview mirror when they stopped for a red light. He saw a car full of guys behind them that looked like the Joe Boys.

Peter leaned forward. "Teddy Bear?"

"Yeah."

"Look slowly in the rearview mirror. Do you recognize the car behind us?"

Teddy Bear looked. "I don't know; I just got out."

Peter leaned back. *He was with street guys who didn't know their own streets.*

There was a car in front of them at the light, their car, and the car with the Joe Boys behind them. "Okay," Peter told Terry, "when the light turns green, let the other car go, then put it in reverse and slam into the car behind us."

"What?" Terry asked.

Peter pulled out his .22 and placed it on the seat next to him. "As soon as the car in front of us is out of the way, slam back."

The light changed. The car ahead moved and Terry jammed the car in reverse, slamming back into the car behind them with a loud crash. Before the people in the car knew what had happened, the Camaro was burning rubber and cut down a side street.

When they knew they weren't being followed, Peter spoke. "This isn't working."

"Hey, we got away; it's working."

"No, I mean this." Peter held up the small .22. "This isn't working. We need bulletproof vests. We need some real guns. We need lots of shit."

The four of them drove to a large hunting store where they could buy bulletproof vests and all the weaponry they needed. As they parked the car, they realized that the shop was full of Joe Boys, all buying the same things they had come to the store for: bulletproof vests, guns, ammo.

After careful consideration, they decided it was time for Danny and Peter to leave. There was *heart*, and then there was—well, whatever this was.

As they headed back to New York, they stopped in Los Angeles so Terry could check in with some other Wah Ching. While waiting for Danny, Peter saw a portrait studio on Sunset Boulevard and walked in. He had the picture taken that appears in this book: sixteen-year-old Peter Chin, cigarette in his mouth, staring at the camera only hours after being shot at by the Joe Boys. Peter thought that someday, when he was an old man, he could look at this photo and remember this trip.

The two drove back to New York in the Camaro that had three bullet holes in it.

Back in the insulated world of New York's Chinatown and its residents, the new status of the Ghost Shadows represented the fall and rise of a government. When residents had issues with their neighbors, landlords, businesses, vendors, and other gangs, they didn't go to the police; they went to those in power. In Chinatown, that power was now held by the Ghost Shadows. Certain names were becoming well known within the Ghost

Shadows. No one knew who Peter Chin was—even Peter rarely thought of himself as that name.

Chinatown was beginning to know Kid Jai.

A middle-aged woman came to see Peter. She was crying as she was escorted in by a Ghost Shadow named Sam, who went by the street name Sasquatch. Peter looked to Sasquatch and then to the crying woman. He waited for her to speak.

"Her name is Jackie," the woman that came to see Peter said, then paused as she shook with sobs. She contained herself after a moment and began speaking again with a little more composure. "Her name is Jackie, she's my daughter and is only fifteen years old." Peter listened to the story of how Jackie was forced by the Flying Dragons to work as a prostitute in one of their massage parlors. Jackie didn't want to do it, her parents didn't want her to do it, but she had tried to escape many times and was always stopped by the Dragons.

Peter listened, thinking about the violence his mother and sisters endured from his father. He got the address on Chrystie Street where the massage parlor was located, and he and Sasquatch headed out.

They didn't have a plan. Two Ghost Shadows driving to Flying Dragons territory, outnumbered and outgunned, to get a fifteen-year-old girl they didn't know out of a locked and heavily guarded building, assuming that the girl actually didn't want to be there and would willingly go with them. Luckily, sometimes things work out better without plans.

They arrived at the building on Chrystie Street and Sasquatch knocked on the front door. There were footsteps, then a voice called out, "Who is it?"

Sasquatch answered, "Kid Jai." They heard the voice behind the door say, "Shit, it's Kid Jai." The door unlocked and swung open.

Peter stuck his .38 in the man's face. Without saying a word, Sasquatch also pointed his gun at the man, holding him there as Peter walked down the dark hallway. Peter began pulling curtains back and asked each young girl the same question: "Are you Jackie? Are you Jackie?" When he finally opened the curtain where the naked girl answered, "Yes, I'm Jackie," he stopped.

Peter asked her his second question. "Do you want to be here?"

She quickly answered, "No," and started to cry.

"Okay, get your clothes on." Voices echoed farther up the hall and Peter realized this would take too long. "No, wrap that blanket around you and let's go."

They raced down the hall and out the front door, away from the footfalls that were coming for them, Sasquatch looking behind. They got Jackie in the car and drove away.

Not a shot was fired.

James Mui became a significant part of Peter Chin's life even though Peter only met him once, in 1976. That one meeting would lead to three arrests, eight months in Rikers Island, two murder charges, an attempt-to-kill-a-witness charge, a shaved head, and a sanitation worker coming to his aid. It all started with a chance meeting on the street.

A street guy can tell another street guy, and there was something about James Mui that Peter picked up on. James was walking with a few others and Peter was walking with a few Ghost Shadows in their territory. They stopped James as they passed him.

"Who the fuck are you?" Peter asked, picking up on the gang swagger of the youth.

"Nobody," James said. "I'm not with anybody," he added quickly, meaning that he wasn't affiliated with any gang. Peter asked for his ID to make sure he was giving them the right name, and James showed his Brooklyn Tech High School ID to confirm that his name was James Mui. It all checked out, but something didn't feel right.

"Okay, but who are you with?" Peter repeated.

"No one," James said. Peter knew this kid was lying: he *was* a street kid, and he was with someone. They roughed James Mui up, and told him to get the fuck off their street. Peter didn't think anything of it at the time, but that meeting would change things.

Nicky walked up to Peter. "C'mon, Kid."

"Where are we going?"

"Bowery Street."

"Bowery Street?" Peter asked.

As the Eagles were losing power, the Flying Dragons were gaining it. When the Ghost Shadows moved to Mott, they gave up their control of Pell Street, and the Flying Dragons took it back, along with Bowery and Doyers Streets. Going to Bowery Street was going straight into Flying Dragons territory.

"My sister is getting married. There's a banquet on Bowery. I want to stop by and have a drink with them."

Peter was uncomfortable with this. "Let me grab a few guys."

"No, just you. We'll be fine."

"Okay, then let me grab a piece at least."

"We'll be fine. We'll only be there for a few minutes." The two of them walked to a restaurant on Bowery Street called Double Happiness, down the street from a Flying Dragons gambling house. Peter was nervous, walking unarmed with the Dai Lo in enemy territory.

Nicky walked inside and Peter waited outside the restaurant's floor-to-ceiling windows. Within minutes, Peter was surrounded by eight Flying Dragons.

There is something that happens when street guys meet street guys. A nonverbal way to acknowledge *I know who you are, and you know who I am*. The only Flying Dragon that spoke was Onionhead, Johnny Eng, a high-ranking member of the Flying Dragons. Peter had never met him but knew his description and immediately recognized him. Onionhead knew that he was talking to Kid Jai.

"What the fuck are you doing here?" Onionhead barked.

"My Dai Lo is inside having a drink with his sister." Peter instinctively reached back for the pistol that wasn't there. "This is her wedding day. One drink and then we'll go."

Peter turned to Nicky inside and gave him a "hurry up" gesture.

As Peter scanned the gang of Flying Dragons surrounding him, he saw a face he recognized: a kid with the street name Fun Bill with whom Peter had gone to elementary school. Peter was surprised that Bill had ended up as a street guy. Later on, Fun Bill would be involved in the assassination of the Flying Dragons' Dai Lo, the Scientist.

Onionhead stared at Peter, then looked inside and saw Nicky getting up from his table.

"Get the fuck off of my street," he growled, walking away. The other Flying Dragons followed.

On the way back to Mott, Peter chastised Nicky. "I told you we should have brought a piece." It amazed Peter how easily Nicky was willing to put his life on the line. There was risk—even walking out your door was risky—but there were actions beyond risk.

James Mui, the boy whom Peter had shaken down and threatened on Mott Street, was actually a member of the Flying Dragons. On April 3, 1976, while Peter Chin was on Mott Street, James Mui and two other Flying Dragons were waiting for a takeout order from the Co-Luck restaurant at 42 Bowery Street. Several Ghost Shadows spotted these Flying Dragons and started firing at them. One bullet hit James Mui in the leg and a few of the other Flying Dragons were injured. A stray bullet went through the window of the Co-Luck and hit thirty-nine-year-old restaurant patron Victoria Kwa, killing her instantly.

When the police asked Mui if he knew who shot at him, he said he did.

"Kid Jai."

It's unclear why James Mui made that statement to the police. It could have been because Peter was the only Ghost Shadow he had contact with, it could have been out of revenge for the beating, or maybe he honestly believed that Peter Chin was one of the shooters.

The police moved in and found Peter coming out of a Mott Street restaurant off Canal Street. He was arrested and booked for homicide and attempted homicide. The reporters believed that he was still fifteen years old, so the articles that appeared in the *Daily News* didn't reveal his name.

Peter Chin returned to Rikers Island.

Rikers was a violent place where racial tensions were high. One time, Peter saw a Caucasian kid waiting to be given a cell. He was sitting in a chair with his blanket, hadn't even been processed yet, and had no beef with anyone yet, but eight African American men suddenly threw a sheet over him and sliced him repeatedly with razors. Peter watched the white sheet change to red. He had been there less than an hour.

Peter Chin got in many fights on Rikers Island. He quickly realized that his long hair was a liability since it could be grabbed and held on to during a fight. Peter shaved his head so that when he got into a fight, the attacker wouldn't have anything to grab. This single act later saved him from a longer prison sentence.

The Ghost Shadow attorneys got to work getting Peter released on bail, and soon he was back on the street.

Once again, some Ghost Shadows spotted a group of Flying Dragons, this time on Pell Street, and began shooting. James Mui was with them and told police that he knew it was Kid Jai. Peter was going to be charged with attempting to murder a witness.

In response to the rise in violent and organized crime activity in Chinatown, the police department had created an elite task force run out of the Fifth Precinct called the Jade Squad. Detective Neil Mauriello was one of the founding members of the squad, working directly with Nancy Ryan of the Manhattan District Attorney's Office to build cases against Chinatown organized crime.

Neil took a unique approach to his job. He knew there was a culture and history involved. Neil integrated himself into Chinatown, talking to gang members, remembering birthdays and events, getting to know them, becoming a part of their community, but also doing his job. As a result, Neil was trusted— as much as a cop capable of arresting you can be—for being fair but tough. Chinatown organized crime hated him, but they also respected him.

Neil Mauriello arrested Peter Chin for the attempted murder of the witness James Mui. In pure Neil Mauriello fashion, he did so in a unique way.

Neil approached Peter. "Kid," he said. "I'm going to arrest you now, but I'm going to give you your dignity and not put you in cuffs."

Peter looked at Neil, trying to determine what he was being charged with.

"You will walk with me over to the Fifth Precinct." Neil extended his arm down the block like he was inviting a friend for a stroll.

"Okay," Peter answered.

"If you try to run," Neil added, "I'll shoot you."

That seemed like a fair trade to Peter.

Peter Chin was arrested, booked, and sent back to Rikers Island. The lawyers couldn't arrange bail this time, but they did hire investigators to work the case. Peter waited in Rikers Island for two to three months until it was time for court. During this time, the investigators uncovered some interesting facts. Peter's attorney stated that at this time of night on Pell Street, it was too dark to possibly identify a face across the street. Two sanitation workers who were on duty the night of the shooting did not see the face of the shooter because it was too dark, but they were certain of one thing: the shooter had long hair.

Peter, having shaved his head during his previous stint in Rikers Island, had short hair.

James Mui was found to be an unreliable witness in the second case of threatening to harm a witness. Since James was the only witness in the first case, the Co-Luck shooting, this case against Peter was also dropped.

With both cases dismissed, Peter Chin was again a free man. In an ironic twist, Peter was walking with a Ghost Shadow named Crazy past city hall only a few weeks later when he saw a few Flying Dragons. In a fit of rage for the eight months he had lost in Rikers Island, Peter pulled out his pistol and started firing blindly. Other than bullets flying into the mayor's office, no one was hit, since Peter was such a bad shot.

The twist here is that Peter was accused of two street shootings that he didn't participate in, but he got away with this one, and others that he did.

While Peter was in Rikers Island for those eight months, Nicky Louie, who had taken the Ghost Shadows further than ever before, made a bad call. His decision drastically decreased their income and dramatically increased public pressure on them, undoing much of their progress.

Man Bun Lee was the unofficial mayor of Chinatown. He was the president of the Chinese Consolidated Benevolent Association, Manhattan's largest civic organization. He was a successful restaurateur, a social and political figure, and a man with important governmental and political ties. Lee founded the Chinatown Manpower Project to provide job training and language classes to immigrants. He converted two buildings in Chinatown on Walker and Mulberry Streets for community use. He was a key driver in the force to create Confucius Plaza, a residence for low-income individuals. In 1976, to honor his civic and social contributions, February 29 was declared Man Bun Lee Day.

Lee was also an ardent opponent of Chinatown organized

crime. He fought it relentlessly: offering counseling services to get youth out of the gangs, speaking against the extortion of business owners, using his power and influence to openly oppose the violence that afflicted New York's Chinatown.

Nicky Louie wanted Man Bun Lee gone, so he hired a hit man to kill him: Chick Keung Pang, a Hong Kong native with ties to West Coast Chinatown organized crime.

On July 11, 1977, Chick Keung Pang went to the Koh Wah restaurant on Mott Street, which Lee owned. Pang located Man Bun Lee, waited until he was in a secluded part of the restaurant, and stabbed him five times.

Man Bun Lee fell to the floor, bleeding profusely, as Pang ran from the restaurant. Man Bun Lee was rushed to the hospital and, although his injuries were life threatening, he survived.

This violence did the opposite of what Nicky Louie hoped. Instead of decreasing public pressure on Chinese organized crime, the pressure multiplied, and not merely on the *gangs* of Chinatown but on the Ghost Shadows specifically.

In an act of pure punishment, Fifth Precinct captain Allan Hoehl decided to hit Nicky Louie and the Ghost Shadows where it hurt: in the wallet. For decades, the police had looked the other way from the gambling houses of Chinatown. The concentration of them on Mott Street was controlled by the Ghost Shadows. The police had taken hush money, they'd accepted bribes, but no longer. For one full year, the gambling houses were to be shut down. One year. If the Ghost Shadows tried to open one, it would be raided and shut down once more.

The spigot producing an endless flow of cash for Nicky Louie and the Ghost Shadows was suddenly turned off. The group abruptly had to survive solely on extortion from the other shop owners on Mott and from any other crimes they could commit.

When Peter returned from Rikers Island, Mott Street gambling houses were dark. The Ghost Shadows were receiving a fraction of the profit they had earned when he went in.

When they had taken over Mott Street, the crown jewel of Chinatown, from the Eagles, the Ghost Shadows made strategic decisions to control it. In order to keep a street, you had to allocate resources to it, so the Ghost Shadows pulled soldiers from Pell Street and the surrounding area to focus on Mott. This move led to the Flying Dragons taking back Pell, which made the defeated Eagles even weaker. The Flying Dragons managed to build their power back up.

The Ghost Shadows had increased dramatically in reputation, power, and numbers, going from fifteen members in 1975 to over seventy by 1977. Suddenly, this bigger organization had more mouths to feed with less money coming in. They were also dealing with a growing rift between two groups within the Ghost Shadows.

There were the street guys—Peter, Mongo, Applehead, Taiwan, Stinky Bug—who were the core of the Ghost Shadows and loyal to the organization. Then there were guys that Nicky had brought in as the gang expanded: Pork Chop, Round Head, Spider. They were loyal to Nicky before the group.

The finances of the Ghost Shadows had severely dwindled; however, Nicky Louie did not seem to notice this economic pinch. This was noticed by a core Ghost Shadow member, Taiwanese Boy, or Taiwan, which led to an incident in a meeting in 1978.

Ghost Shadow meetings weren't uncommon. Nicky Louie called them occasionally to discuss where he needed resources. Sometimes meetings were important, other times they were routine. This particular meeting looked like it would be a routine one.

"I'll be a little late," Peter told Mongo. "I'll miss the beginning of the meeting, but I'll be there before it's over."

"Late?" Mongo asked. "Why?"

"I'll be coming in from Queens."

"Queens?" Mongo looked at Peter with curiosity. "What's in Queens?"

"*She* is in Queens." Peter smiled, referring to a girl he'd met.

Mongo grinned, and Peter went to Queens. On his way back to Mott Street while Peter was still on the Manhattan Bridge, something was occurring in the meeting that would change the Ghost Shadows forever.

While pulling his car onto Mott, Peter saw Mongo, Taiwan, Applehead, and Stinky Bug on the street, not on the third floor where the meeting was supposed to be taking place.

This can't be good, Peter thought. He parked the car and approached the other Ghost Shadows.

"All I did was ask to see the books," Taiwan told Peter. "We're not seeing the money we had. I wanted to see what money we did have and where it was going."

"Okay. What did he say?"

"He didn't say anything," Taiwan insisted. "He had that guy, Spider, put a gun to my head."

Peter listened. Taiwan had requested to see the Ghost Shadows' books. Not an unrealistic request. The normal response would have been for Nicky to show them and answer any questions Taiwan had, not to threaten him. In doing so, Nicky had turned on his own guy, one who had been with him since they'd taken over Mott Street.

"He wants to split," said Mongo. "We have one side of Mott and he and his guys have the other."

"*His* guys? We're all *his* guys."

Peter knew that a split like that wouldn't work. Why wasn't Nicky trying to work this out with Taiwan?

In the outside world, there would be more discussion before such a major decision. On the Chinatown streets, there's a different, faster process. You looked at what the next move against you might be and considered what you could do to defend against it. Within minutes, it was clear what was happening.

Nicky was going to kill Taiwan, which meant that Nicky was choosing power, and himself, over the Ghost Shadows. Nicky had to go.

"Let's get the guns," Peter said.

There was a stash of guns nearby, and Applehead rushed to them, but Nickie and his group had beat them to it.

"This is all that was left." Applehead held a .22 long pistol and a two-shot derringer. Peter took the .22 and another Ghost Shadow, Pipenose, took the derringer.

While Peter and his group were organizing, Nicky Louie and his group were doing the same. The shoot-out that happened next occurred quickly.

Nicky's group was running, and Peter's group fired at them. Peter rapidly emptied all five rounds at Nicky at close range, half a block, and missed every time. Nicky's group fired back, forcing Mongo, Taiwan, Applehead, and Peter to separate.

Seeking shelter, Peter and Pipenose ran to a small gambling house on the corner of Bayer and Mott.

"You." Peter pointed to the old gambling house doorman. "Get out of the way. He'll watch the door." Peter stationed Pipenose at the door to ensure that none of Nicky's guys got in. He checked the back for another way out of the gambling house, since in Mock Duck's day there were tunnels. The tunnels had since been filled in.

Peter and Pipenose were safe for now, but they were trapped inside the gambling house with an empty gun and Nicky's guys right outside.

A few minutes later, the gambling house phone rang. The doorman answered it.

"Kid," the older doorman said. "It's for you. It's Nicky."

"Hang up," Kid ordered. The doorman did.

Five minutes passed, and the phone rang again. Peter took the call.

Nicky spoke first. "We need to talk this over, Kid."

Talk this over? Peter thought. *That's good. Maybe this whole mess can be fixed.*

"Nicky, you come in here unarmed. If you do, I'll guarantee your safety. I'll have a gun on you the entire time."

"You give me your word?"

"Yes."

Peter looked out the peephole of the gambling house to see Nicky walking down the stairs to the entrance. He had his shirt lifted up so Peter could see he was unarmed. Peter spoke through the closed door.

"Turn around." Nicky complied.

When Peter opened the door, he kept his empty pistol trained on Nicky, who had his hands raised. *He doesn't know it's empty,* Peter knew. They entered the gambling house and Pipenose closed the door behind them, locking it.

"I want you on my side, Kid," Nicky said.

"Your side? We're all on the same side."

"Not anymore."

As they talked, it became clear to Peter that Nicky wanted to thin the herd. Nicky wanted to take out anyone who questioned the money Nicky was taking or his authority to take it. They weren't the Ghost Shadows anymore. They weren't those twelve guys who took over Mott Street. This was the robbing of the robbers, stealing from the people Nicky had once called brothers.

"You can still work this out, Nicky. Talk to Taiwan."

"That part is over, Kid. Will you join me or not?"

Peter felt a sadness wash over him. The Ghost Shadows had gone from bad days to good days together—why would this have to end now, like this? How could one hand go against the other? Nicky was the leader, he was supposed to solve problems, not create them. He was supposed to take care of their family.

"You and I are going to leave here, Nicky. I know your guys are outside. I will have this gun to your back. If they try and stop me, I'll kill you."

"Kid, join my side."

Peter gripped Nicky's arm as they walked outside and up the steps, Peter using Nicky to shield himself as they stepped into the street.

"Don't shoot!" Nicky yelled to his men. Peter backed Nicky down the street, to the corner, then let him go and ran. He caught a cab that took him where the Ghost Shadows went if they were ever separated in a shoot-out: Times Square. When he arrived, the four other generals were waiting for him: Mongo, Taiwan, Applehead, and Stinky Bug.

They talked. They planned. These five generals decided that there would no longer be just one Dai Lo of the Ghost Shadows. They, the five generals, would rule together; they would be the new Dai Lo: Kid Jai, Mongo, Applehead, Stinky Bug, and Taiwan.

First, they had to kill Nicky Louie. They were all in danger with Nicky alive.

"Okay," Peter said. "I'll do it." Peter knew that because he was such a bad shot, he'd have to get in close to do it.

Nicky Louie had been gone for several weeks and Mott Street was divided. There were the traditional Ghost Shadows consisting of the five generals and about fifty others, and then there were Nicky's Ghost Shadows, around twenty older guys. One group was on one side of Mott Street. One group was on the other.

"It's just a matter of time." Mongo looked at the group on the other side. "Someone has to make the first move."

"It's Nicky we need," Peter responded. "When he goes down, they'll scatter."

Nicky had been staying away. It wasn't until August 29, 1978, that he resurfaced. Stinky Bug saw him.

"Is he hiding?" Peter asked. "How many guys does he have?"

"No, he's alone." Stinky Bug smiled. "And he's not hiding, he's gambling. Right here on Mott."

Nicky gambling alone after the Ghost Shadows had tried to

kill him only weeks before was either the ballsiest or the stupidest thing Peter had ever heard.

The Gin Beck restaurant was on Mott Street. Underneath it was a barbershop, and behind that, a hidden mahjong gambling table where Nicky liked to play. Depending on where Nicky was sitting, it should be pretty easy to get to him.

"Okay," Peter said. "I'll take care of it."

Before he could get down the street, Robert Hsu, who went by the street name Potato and was a loyal Ghost Shadow, stopped him. "Let me do it," Potato said. "I know he was your friend. I can do it."

"I can do it." Peter tried to step around him. "It has to be done right."

"I can do it, Kid." Potato took the .38 from Peter's hand. "Let me do it."

Peter considered it. "Are you sure?"

"Yes."

"Okay, but you have to do it right, Potato. Two or three in the head. No fucking around."

"I've got it."

Potato walked down Mott and down the stairs of number 17, the back way through the barbershop. When he reached the ground level, he saw four people at the mahjong table. Sitting with his back toward Potato, in front of an open sliding door, was Nicky. Potato crept forward, slid the door open, and raised the gun. The player opposite Nicky happened to look up and saw Potato walking toward them with a gun. This player's face reacted, just for a second, which was enough time for Nicky to respond and move slightly to the left as Potato fired the gun. The first shot hit the side of Nicky's face, while the other three bullets hit him in the back. Potato ran back up the steps and out of the building.

When he got back to Peter, he relayed what had happened.

"He's got to be dead," Potato said, panting. "I shot him in the head and the back."

Kid listened. He wanted to believe Potato, but something

didn't feel right. As Potato was repeating the story to Peter for the third time, a gravely injured Nicky was making his way to the Fifth Precinct, which was only a block away. From there, he was transported to Beekman Downtown Hospital, where he remained in a coma for several days.

The New York newspapers reported that Nicky Louie would pull through, that he'd used up another of his nine lives.

Back on Mott Street, word got out that Nicky Louie had been shot. By the end of the day, Nicky's Ghost Shadow faction that manned the other side of the street was gone. The Ghost Shadows were one again.

After weighing his options, Nicky agreed to be a cooperating witness against the very group he had once led.

At the time, Nicky had no pending cases against him. He had no reason to name Potato for leniency toward a case. No deal was struck with him to do so. However, Nicky decided to name Potato in the shooting. He was cooperating, but he wasn't getting anything out of it. Potato was arrested and sentenced to five to fifteen years for the attempted murder of Nicky Louie.

Nicky left New York to try his luck in Chicago.

Peter Chin has always been good with faces. Even after years of not seeing someone, if their face is locked into Peter's memory, he always recognizes them.

Peter was walking on Canal between the south end of Mott with three other Ghost Shadows when he recognized someone on the other side of the street, a face he hadn't seen for six years. Peter rapidly instructed the group and soon encircled the man. As if they'd rehearsed it, one Ghost Shadow taking one arm and one Ghost Shadow taking the other, they grabbed him and steered him toward Mott Street.

The man panicked at first, saw that he was outnumbered, then didn't struggle further. They brought him to a basement Ghost Shadow hideout and forced him into a chair.

Peter stepped in front of him.

"Do you remember me?" Peter asked, leaning in so the man could see his face.

"No." The man's voice was shaking.

"Maybe you remember a twelve-year-old kid that you and your friend beat and robbed? And not just a little, you *really* beat the shit out of this kid, and he only had two quarters on him."

The blood drained out of the man's face as his eyes widened in recognition. Peter gave the signal and the beating began. Peter began to lecture.

"What made you think a twelve-year-old kid would have anything more than fifty cents?"

There was a punch to the right eye, the gut, the nose.

"It doesn't make any sense."

A punch to the lower lip, then one that broke the nose, then another gut punch that broke a rib.

"You'd be better off waiting outside a bank for a well-dressed guy to walk out and then following and jumping him. At least he'd have *something*."

Kicks were added, then more punching. The man's ear started bleeding.

"Instead, you went for the weakest person you could find. That makes you a coward."

A punch, a kick, a punch.

"It doesn't make any fuckin' sense."

Peter gave the signal and the beating stopped. The man's face was unrecognizable.

"Do you still see your friend? The other guy?" The man nodded. "I want you to go find him and show him your face. Tell him if I see him again, or if I hear that you two beat on kids, this will happen to him. The next time I see you, it will be worse."

The Ghost Shadows released the man's arms, allowing him to slump back in the chair. "Be better thieves from now on. I don't think you're very good at it."

*   *   *

In 1977, after three years in the psychiatric hospital, Peter's mother, Kiu Chin, was released. Nancy Chin visited her mother at the hospital every day. Kiu would eat only Chinese food, and if Nancy didn't bring some for her, her mother would go hungry. Nancy was excited by Kiu's progress and proud that their mother could come home.

Nancy had been busy herself. She and her boyfriend, David, had gotten married, saved every penny, and opened a small garment factory on the outskirts of Chinatown. When their mother was released, Kiu could work there with Nancy, where she could keep an eye on her mom.

"Let me get you a place to live," Peter said to his mother over the phone. "Even a house. Give me a few days to—"

"I have a place to live," she answered. "With my husband."

Peter knew this was coming. Nancy had warned him. He knew that after Bark broke her arm, beat her children, tried to stab her son with a knife, and drove her to three years in a psychiatric hospital, Kiu still upheld her marital vows.

Kiu moved back into the apartment at 92 East Broadway with Bark, the Cow. Peter was frustrated and angry at his father, but he focused on Chinatown, which was undergoing changes of its own.

Peter Wong was not a gangster but someone who *knew people.* Peter Wong was on the fringe. From this fringe, in 1978 he saw an incredible opportunity: If the gambling houses were to be closed for a year, then who better to open one than a fringe guy, someone not attached to the Ghost Shadows? Owning the only open gambling house in Chinatown was a once-in-a-lifetime opportunity.

Peter Wong found a place on Baxter Street, where Walker became Canal Street, and opened a gambling house. The local police, seeing that it was independent of the Ghost Shadows, let it slide. Peter Wong became successful very quickly. Being only the second gambling house in Chinatown—Uncle Benny's gambling house was still open; even the police wouldn't close that—where there had been fifteen only months before, it attracted all the gangs, each wanting a piece.

Peter Wong knew the rules. He had no problem paying for protection, but he wanted to pay one group a set amount, not the constantly rising fee that each group asked. He wanted real protection from whomever he paid.

Peter Wong went to Kid Jai and asked for his help. If the two of them could keep the Ghost Shadows relationship quiet, if Kid Jai could straighten it out with the other gangs so there was one protection payment, this could be profitable. Kid Jai agreed. The other gangs backed off, and the one gambling house in all of Chinatown opened and quickly flourished.

Over time, Peter Chin and Peter Wong became friends. One day, out of nowhere, Peter Wong asked an interesting question.

"If anything were to happen to me, would you look after my family?"

Peter Chin was surprised. "What's going to happen to you?"

"Nothing. I just wanted to know that if something did, you know, my family would be okay."

Kid Jai smiled. "Yeah, I would."

With the success of the gambling house and Peter Wong's other businesses, it's unclear why the fake shark fin robbery happened. It wasn't for money, it wasn't for power, and it didn't end well for Peter Wong. Perhaps it occurred as a way for Peter Wong to pay back Kid Jai for his help, but this is unclear.

Peter Wong had an idea. In 1979 Chinatown, shark fin was a rare delicacy. Restaurants were paying around $45 a pound. In comparison, lobster was selling at about $3 a pound. Peter Wong had a lot of freeze-dried shark fin coming in and he told Kid Jai to come take it so Peter Wong could pretend he was robbed.

"Okay." Peter Chin was confused. "What do you want for your part?"

"Nothing." Peter Wong shrugged. "Only make sure you take my watch and jewelry, too, so I can say they were taken during the robbery. You can give them back to me later."

Peter Chin was uncomfortable with this division of profits and asked several more times what Peter Wong wanted for his cut. The answer was always the same. *Nothing, but make sure to take my watch and jewelry.*

In preparation, Peter Chin rented an apartment in Brooklyn to store the shark fin, along with a few vans for transport. On July 19, 1979, the fake shark fin robbery occurred. Peter Chin and crew arrived, took the shark fin and the jewelry, and left. Wong did his part by telling everyone that he had been robbed and how the robbers had even taken his personal jewelry.

The plan seemed to be working. Inquiries were made, parties were frustrated, but life continued. A few weeks later, Peter Wong began wearing the same jewelry that Peter Chin had returned to him.

This was noticed by more and more people until Peter Wong was summoned by Uncle Benny himself. Peter Wong went, stuck to his story, and left.

If Uncle Benny had known that Kid Jai was involved, there would have been options, or at least further conversations, but Peter Wong was an outsider and there were rules for outsiders. Uncle Benny sanctioned a hit on Peter Wong.

On February 13, 1980, Peter Wong was leaving the nightclub he owned. He got in his car, but it wouldn't start, which was strange because the car had been running fine just a few hours earlier. Peter Wong stepped out of the car and opened the hood. A witness saw a cab pull up alongside the car and roll down the window.

"Peter Wong," the driver said, more of a statement than a question.

"Yeah?" Peter Wong turned. The driver of the cab shot Peter Wong in the face.

There were very few gangs in Chinatown that had cab licenses. The Flying Dragons were one of them; therefore, it's most likely that Uncle Benny gave the contract to kill Peter Wong to the Flying Dragons.

Although this is *officially* still a cold case, it is Peter Chin's opinion that Peter Wong was killed by a man named Liang Jai, who went by the street name Youngest. Youngest would also be involved in another hit that would trigger a chain reaction that would alter Chinatown forever.

Peter Chin now had two things to take care of: Peter Wong's family, whom he had vowed to look after, and three rooms full of shark fin.

Without Peter Wong around, his gambling house eventually closed. By then, the year moratorium was ending. Testing the waters, the Ghost Shadows opened a gambling house. When the police didn't raid it, they opened another, then another, until Chinatown was filled with illegal gambling houses once again.

"You've got to see him," Stinky Bug insisted.

"A fortune teller?" Peter mocked. "C'mon."

Stinky Bug wouldn't give up. After all, this wasn't just a fortune teller—he was the most famous psychic in all of Hong Kong.

"He is Li Ka Shing's personal fortune teller," Stinky Bug said. "That guy is a billionaire. Shing won't make a move without talking to this guy first."

Peter was unimpressed. "I don't believe in that shit." Stinky Bug would not give up.

"He's only here on vacation," he explained. "He may never be in New York again and he can meet us in an apartment on Mulberry."

Peter tried to get out of it, but Stinky Bug wouldn't let it go. Peter reluctantly agreed to meet with the fortune teller.

The two walked to the apartment on Mulberry, and the psychic sat with Peter, staring at him. Then he spoke.

"You have two hurdles," the fortune teller said. "One will occur soon, within a year. This hurdle will be hard and you may not survive it. The other hurdle will be even more difficult, but this won't occur until you are seventy-two years old. In between these two hurdles is a world of wealth for you. More money than you can spend in three lifetimes. Spend it well before the second hurdle."

The two Ghost Shadows left the apartment on Mulberry.

"Wow," Stinky Bug said. "You're going to be rich."

"Or dead in a year," Peter added.

"If you survive, you'll live rich until you're seventy-two. That's old."

"If you believe that shit." Peter lit a cigarette. "Which I don't."

In a secret ceremony in April 1979, Peter Chin and Ida May Wong were married. There was no announcement and no banquet, and only Peter's immediate family and Mongo knew. The couple moved into an apartment in Brooklyn, away from Chinatown, and Peter wore no wedding ring. In order to keep his wife safe, Peter kept her a secret, hidden from the enemies of the Ghost Shadows.

In the same year, Mongo and Applehead, two of the five generals, were convicted in a large extortion case in Baltimore. They each received a sixteen-year sentence. Taiwanese Boy, who was also involved, decided to take his chances on the run, becoming a fugitive. This meant that of the five generals who acted as the group Dai Lo for the past two years, only two remained: Kid Jai and Stinky Bug.

Having two people making major decisions for the Ghost Shadows seemed more complicated than having a committee of five do it, so it was decided that the captains of the Ghost Shadows would vote to determine who would be the official leader. Kid Jai won. This angered Stinky Bug, who said that he would leave the Ghost Shadows. Peter worked hard to get him to change his mind.

"I'll be Dai Lo in name only," Peter said. "I'll run everything through you, and we'll lead together."

Stinky Bug wasn't having it. Peter spent hours trying to talk Stinky Bug into staying, begged him, but it didn't work.

"I want nothing more to do with you, or the Ghost Shadows," Stinky Bug said. "Ever."

Peter reluctantly gave in.

"I won't come against you, Stinky Bug," Peter said. "You can leave, and you won't have to look over your shoulder for me. Just don't form another group or come for me."

Stinky Bug agreed. He left the Ghost Shadows and Peter became Dai Lo.

Stinky Bug's promise lasted six months. He formed a group in Queens called the White Tigers. This bothered Peter, who saw the move as a violation of the agreement and of his trust, but he let it go. Until the White Tigers shot at a group of Ghost Shadows. The Ghost Shadows returned fire and then more shootings and attacks occurred. This incited war.

The White Tigers were now the enemy of the Ghost Shadows. Since the White Tigers were taking territory from existing organizations, they became the enemy of the Flying Dragons as well.

Even though Mongo and Applehead were still in prison, Peter collected their financial cut every week and gave it to their families. Taiwan, who remained a fugitive, was hiding in plain sight in Queens. Peter brought him his cut in secret.

On January 15, 1980, after returning from seeing Taiwan, Peter saw two men running down Mott Street whom he didn't recognize. They were being chased by a group of Flying Dragons. Peter intercepted the Flying Dragons.

"What the fuck you doing on my street?"

"Those guys are White Tigers." They pointed to the two men running to the next block.

"We'll take care of it," Peter said. "Just get the fuck off my street."

The Flying Dragons left and the Ghost Shadows caught up to the two men, dragged them under a bridge, beat them, then shot them in the head.

It was later revealed that these two men were not connected to the White Tigers, or to any of the gangs. Any new faces in Chinatown were assumed to be White Tigers, and these kids had made the mistake of running when the Flying Dragons yelled at them. They were innocent civilians who were killed because Peter was given bad information.

Shortly after this, Anthony, Peter Chin's son, was born. Like the wedding and Peter's family, Anthony was kept a secret.

CHAPTER 5
The Golden Taipei

Fu Man brushed rain from his sleeves and closed the door behind him. "Kid, I have something that could be good for you."

"Okay." Peter was pretending to read the invoices on his desk. He was embarrassed that he couldn't read them in either English or Cantonese. His one day of school in Hong Kong taught him the same amount as the five years of elementary school in the United States—nothing. If he couldn't do it, he had to find someone who could. *I need guys who can hold a pen,* he thought, *and not just a gun. I need a few educated guys with me.*

Fu Man was one of those pen holders, a Ghost Shadow who could read and speak both English and Cantonese. They needed more like him.

"Do you know Tony Chun?" Fu Man asked

"No." Peter piled the invoices into bins by color.

"He's with United Bamboo."

United Bamboo was a Taiwanese Triad with a small presence in New York. There were around a dozen of them in the city.

Peter looked up. "I know most of the United Bamboo guys, but don't know him."

"Well, he's got a club he wants to sell you."

"Club? What kind of club?"

"A nightclub on Forty-Sixth Street."

The idea of someone he didn't know wanting to sell him a nightclub concerned Peter. If it was a profitable club, why sell it? If it had value, why not sell it to a friend or someone you knew? If it was anything good, why bring him in on it? A stranger. The only time you sold a stranger a club would be if it had hidden problems, such as vendors who hadn't been paid, liquor licenses that were about to be revoked, or hidden partnerships. Curiosity got the better of Peter, and he agreed to meet with the owner.

The nightclub on Forty-Sixth Street and Seventh Avenue was called Golden Taipei. When Peter and Sasquatch walked in, they expected it to be small like most Chinese nightclubs in Manhattan. Like the Mayflower, where Nei Wong was killed. This space was large, with a winding bar and tables spread around a dance floor. It opened up to a restaurant, allowing people to flow from the restaurant into the club.

What's wrong with it? Peter wondered.

The club was largely empty, which seemed strange because it had a great flow of street traffic. The location was perfect. The only customers were sitting where several tables were pushed together. About fourteen guys were drinking and talking loudly. The owner, Tony, came out from the back and showed them around the club.

They sat down, and Peter asked his questions. "Do you owe on liquor?" The answer was no. "Are the taxes paid up? What is the status of the vendors you work with?" Peter received the satisfactory answers he wanted.

Tony knew the question Peter really wanted to ask, so he lowered his voice and leaned in. "It's them!" Tony nodded toward the large table of loud people. "They are the problem."

Tony explained that this group came in regularly, expected to drink on the house, rang up huge bills, never paid for food, got drunk, and scared away any good business. "No one will come here because of them."

"That's the only problem with the place?"

"Yes," Tony answered.

Okay, Peter thought, *I can take care of that problem.*

A man pushed himself away from the large table and stumbled toward them. He wobbled to a stop in front of Peter.

"Brother Kid?"

Peter looked at the man's bloodshot eyes. "Do I know you?" Peter asked, annoyed that his conversation was being interrupted.

"My name is Wise Guy, Brother Kid. I would like to have a drink with you."

Peter sized him up. He was connected—Peter wasn't sure to whom, Flying Dragons maybe—but probably not too far up the chain. "No disrespect, Wise Guy, but I'm not much of a drinker and I'm talking to this man right now."

Wise Guy's face went from contentment to anger and he turned, heading back to the table. Peter saw someone pass him a pistol.

Peter leaned over to Sasquatch. "Go use the pay phone in the hotel lobby and call Mott Street. Have them send a few guys over."

Sasquatch went. Peter continued talking to Tony, and they struck a deal: $50,000 and the club would change hands. Peter would give Tony half now, and half when he picked up the keys. The two men shook hands.

As Peter got up to leave, Wise Guy ambled back toward Peter and reached for his pistol. Peter quickly stuck his own pistol in Wise Guy's face.

"If you pull that gun out any farther, Wise Guy, I'll blow your head off."

Two arms reached around Wise Guy and pinned his arms down. Wise Guy yelled and squirmed to get away.

"No disrespect, Kid Jai," the man holding Wise Guy said. "It's his birthday today; he just drank too much, that's all."

"Who are you?" Peter asked.

"No one, Kid. My name is Paul, they call me Fuk Chow Paul, but I'm not connected to anyone. Wise Guy is not himself. He's sorry."

"Okay, Paul, take him back to his table." Peter put his pistol back. "Enjoy the rest of the night. Don't come back to this place again, any of you. I own this place now, and if he is here after tonight, he'll get hurt."

Paul nodded, and the men went back to their table.

Paul, who had the street name of Fuk Chow Paul, may have been a nobody then, but he later became the founder of the Fuk Ching street gang.

Peter took over the club. Wise Guy and his friends stopped coming, and the place was soon filled with customers. Peter rented an apartment across the street from the Golden Taipei so he could be there when needed.

One night, Peter got a call from Sasquatch.

"Hey, that guy you kicked out, Wise Guy, he's back, he's pretty drunk, and he's demanding free drinks."

Peter and some other Ghost Shadows went to the bar, grabbed Wise Guy, pulled him into the kitchen, and forced him down in a chair.

"I guess you didn't understand my message," Peter said, and they proceeded to give Wise Guy a beating severe enough that he had to go to the hospital.

Wise Guy recovered, but he liked to be seen in nightclubs and wanted to make a name for himself. Though he never went back to Peter's club, there was another Asian club in Manhattan. The club was the Sam Bow, a Korean club on Forty-Fifth Street and Sixth Avenue, right behind the Golden Taipei.

About two months after receiving his beating from Peter and the Ghost Shadows, Wise Guy was at the Sam Bow nightclub with Dice. A waiter told Wise Guy that there was a call for him at the pay phone. Wise Guy went to take his call. He was shot in the back of the head while picking up the phone. It was obviously a planned hit, but it was never clear who the order came from.

The Golden Taipei became a very busy and very profitable nightclub, largely because in that part of Manhattan there were only two Asian clubs: Sam Bow and the Golden Taipei. That's why seeing a white face there was unusual.

This face was not only white, but Peter noticed that he was older than the normal crowd. The man sat at the bar and sipped his wine as two Asian men, somewhat intoxicated, started making fun of him. "You might be in the wrong club, Grandpa."

Peter didn't like this. He walked over to the men and told them they could apologize, then leave. They immediately did.

The older man smiled. "It's not their fault. They aren't used to people as handsome as I am."

"That must be it." Peter smiled back.

"I'm Nick," he said. "Can I buy you a drink?"

"Peter." They shook hands. "I own this place, so you don't have to buy me anything."

"Oh," Nick said. "Then how about a little conversation?"

Peter and Nick talked. Peter learned that Nick had a driver waiting for him outside. He came to this bar often because he did a little loan-sharking, and this was a good place for clients to make drops. Nick thanked Peter and left.

Almost every week after that, Nick showed up, and he and Peter talked. Nick said a lot about himself by the things he didn't say, such as, "Peter, when you come into my booth to say hello, do me a favor and don't bring your pistol."

Which meant that Nick was a felon, probably on parole, and being caught with someone with a firearm would be a violation. Peter knew enough about the Italian Mafia to know that Nick was well connected, and by the names he mentioned, the family he belonged to was the Genoveses.

Peter and Nick became friends. "If you're ever in this part of the city"—Nick slid his business card across the table—"please stop by."

Peter looked at the business card, which had the Blimpie Subs logo on it and an address on Thirty-Third Street and Eighth Avenue, which was near Madison Square Garden.

"I will," Peter said, sticking the card in his wallet.

A few months later, Peter and his wife were walking around that area near Madison Square Garden. This reminded Peter of Nick's card in his wallet, so he decided to swing by.

Peter expected to walk into a small dark office, but it was a large, well-furnished waiting room filled with men in suits waiting to see Nick. Peter told the receptionist who he was. She said she would tell Nick he was there and to have a seat.

Before Peter and Ida had a chance to sit, Nick exited his office with another man in tow. "We'll do this some other time," he told the other man. "As you can see, my godson is here."

All the men in the reception area looked at this Asian couple, and that Nick had called one of them "godson," noting they were being brought into his office without waiting. From that point on, Nick introduced Peter to everyone as his godson—Christmas parties, dinners, everywhere.

Peter and Nick started to do business together. Nick was used to the 3 percent vig that money on the streets was getting. Peter was getting 10 percent in Chinatown on a weekly basis. He took a $1 million investment of Nick's money and turned it into $6 million in only sixteen months—$4 million for Nick and $2 million for Peter.

The godfather and the Ghost Shadow became close as they became successful.

In the quest to find more men who could hold a pen rather than a gun, Peter found Jimmy Wong, a blackjack hustler who had gotten in a little trouble with Mongo, which Peter had to step in to smooth over. Jimmy became Peter's translator, and then his driver.

In Chinatown there were three basic categories of people. First were the street guys: hardened, alert, cautious people like

Peter and Mongo, who never turned off, never let their guard down, because they knew what the streets really were.

Then there were the fringe people like Peter Wong, semi-cautious about how dangerous the world around them was. They knew it was an unsafe place, but mostly they remained unwary. They weren't connected or protected, but they knew people who were.

Street hustlers made up the third category. These were the guys who played in a dangerous world but never truly understood that life on the street is a life where caution is always necessary. They never saw the true danger or the true cost. Jimmy Wong was one of those street hustler guys.

Jimmy never seemed to realize where he was, and his view of Chinatown was the opposite of Peter's. Peter Chin was a street guy who knew that if given the opportunity, there were plenty of people trying to kill him. He kept his family secret and protected, on constant alert to see who the people around him were.

When Peter went to get a haircut, the owner of the barbershop would see Kid Jai coming and have all customers wait outside. He closed the barbershop with only Kid Jai and two of his guys inside and then closed the solid metal security gate to protect anyone from seeing, or shooting, inside. Then Peter got his haircut.

When Peter went to eat, he sat at a table facing the door, with one guy at each exit. At a movie theater, he was in the back row, with guys stationed all around. When driving, he looked at the car ahead of and behind him to see if the driver was the type to block him in. He and the Ghost Shadows had far too many people who wanted them gone. Everyone had to be considered an enemy. Jimmy didn't see the world like this.

Jimmy drove Peter around in Jimmy's big Lincoln Mark V. It was a car that stood out on the streets of Chinatown, like he was driving to church.

"Jimmy?" Peter asked.

"Yeah?" Jimmy said, trying to get the radio dial to pick up a good station.

"Didn't you see that car that just turned around?"

"What car?"

"Those were Flying Dragons in that car. They saw us, then turned a sharp right. Get off this street."

Jimmy did. When Peter was with him, Peter had to be alert for both of them. That was a small price to pay, because Jimmy was a good kid and Peter liked him, so much so that Peter wanted to set him up and give him a little bit of independence.

Godfather Nick had given Peter a place to use on West Thirty-Eighth Street, three blocks from Macy's, between Sixth and Seventh Avenues. The plan was to open a blackjack gambling house there and have Jimmy run it, while he and Peter split the profits. They moved the tables in and got the place ready. Jimmy was to meet Peter at 2:00 p.m. to pick up $40,000 to be used for the gambling house. For all Jimmy's flaws, he was never late.

Peter, Jimmy, and Peter's wife Ida had dinner together. As they were leaving, Jimmy passed in the other direction.

"Where are you going?" Peter asked.

"I'm going to go gamble for a while."

"Don't forget to pick me up."

Two o'clock went by. Then three. At four, Peter took a cab to Chinatown to check on the new gambling house.

Seeing a Brooklyn cop in Chinatown was unusual. Brooklyn was a different police jurisdiction, so Peter didn't know all the cops, but he knew the one in front of him named Smitty. When Smitty saw Peter, the cop walked up and showed him a photo of Jimmy, shot, in the front seat of the Mark V.

"Do you know this guy?" Smitty asked.

Peter looked at the photo and his heart stopped. He didn't let his face change. "No, I don't know him."

Smitty explained that Jimmy got boxed in at a light, the car behind him opened fire, Jimmy's foot hit the accelerator, and he crashed into a pole.

Peter listened and tried to look uninterested. *At least he didn't see it coming.* Peter smiled, thinking that Jimmy's final few minutes were probably spent trying to find a good song on the radio.

As soon as Peter saw Dice's face, he knew that Dice was there for more money.

"It's been stressful here lately," Dice explained. "I need to get back to Hong Kong for a while."

"To gamble another $350,000?" Peter asked.

Dice froze and Peter let the silence build. Dice's father was connected to a small but powerful crime family in Hong Kong. Borrowing $350,000 using his father's name wasn't difficult in the opulence of that country. It bothered Peter that Dice blew that much money on gambling instead of using it to build up a business.

"Oh, you thought I didn't know about that?" Peter smiled. "I have friends in Macau. A lot of them."

"Okay," Dice said. "Yeah, okay, I had a bad run, but I just need a little, you know, some money for the plane ticket and everything."

The two talked. Dice made promises. Peter counted off money for Dice to go back to Hong Kong.

"This is the second plane ticket I will buy for you." Peter held out the money. "There won't be a third."

The Ghost Shadows grew the first year Peter was the sole Dai Lo. Many new faces came in, and once they proved themselves, Peter assigned them to key captain positions. These men became incredibly loyal to Peter, who, besides running the Ghost Shadows, was also working on two special projects with the Ghost Shadows' house attorney, Daniel Gotlin.

The two projects involved finding a way to get Applehead and Mongo off with shorter sentences, as well as getting Taiwan out of hiding.

Attorney Gotlin made a deal for Taiwan. If he turned himself in, Gotlin had a quick bail hearing set, a deal made, and Taiwan would be released the same day on a $5,000 bail.

"I'll have my guy waiting at the courthouse with the money as soon as the bail is set," Peter said. "You'll be out that day."

Taiwan didn't like this plan. If the bail hearing took too long, they would transfer him to Rikers Island, and getting bail from there could take hours or longer. Plus, there was a part of Taiwan that wondered if this was a trap set by Kid Jai—that there was no deal and Taiwan would turn himself in to be locked up for sixteen years. After all, this would be a great way for Kid Jai to get rid of Taiwan and have everything for himself. Taiwan had a very suspicious side; in fact, he was the only one of the five generals who no one knew where he lived.

"Let me do this for you," Peter insisted.

After hours of discussing it, Taiwan reluctantly agreed. Taiwan and Gotlin walked into the police station and Taiwan turned himself in. They saw a judge immediately, bail was set, bail was posted, and soon Taiwan was back out on the street.

Peter introduced Taiwan to the new Ghost Shadow crew, but it bothered Taiwan that Peter's new men were so loyal to him. The first order of business was for Taiwan to remove Peter's people from key captain positions and replace them with Taiwan's own handpicked men.

"We're going to starve," Peter's ex-captains complained. "We count on that weekly gambling money and now it's gone."

"It will all work out," Peter reassured them. Life in Chinatown moved on.

In the early morning of April 24, 1980, around six thirty in the morning, Peter was about to turn onto Canal, the dividing line between Chinatown and Little Italy, when he saw five Ghost Shadows beating two men. Peter had a rule not to make trouble on one of their own streets, so he stopped.

"What the fuck are you doing?" Peter asked.

The Ghost Shadows explained that these men were Tong On, and they were on their street.

"When we asked what they was doing here," the Ghost Shadows explained, "they started talking shit to us."

The explanation seemed fair to Peter, so he allowed the beating to continue and got back in the car.

Later that morning, a phone call came in for Peter. It was from Clifford Wong. Peter knew Clifford back from the car service days on Henry Street. Since then, Clifford had risen in rank to become the head of the Tong On. There was a long history of fighting between the Tong On and the Ghost Shadows, and Clifford was upset at how his men had been treated that morning. A heated conversation followed.

A *red envelope* was a term that meant one side asked for forgiveness from the other, a sign of respect, by giving an envelope with cash to the offended party. Peter realized early in the conversation that Clifford was asking for a red envelope, an apology.

"Your guys were in the wrong, Clifford," Peter said. "They were on our street and then started talking shit without any respect for our turf. "

The call ended. Peter felt uneasy, but he shrugged it off and continued with his day.

Mott Street is a very narrow street. There is rarely a place to park if you don't double park, and on that rainy day, that's what Peter did. With two wheels on the sidewalk and two wheels on the street, Peter dashed from his car through the rain to a Ghost Shadow building. As he ran, Peter's street sense picked up a man in a raincoat across the street standing under an awning. Something wasn't right about this man. Peter had never seen him before, and the man was just looking—or more accurately, trying to seem like he was *not* looking—at Peter.

Peter walked upstairs to the safe house, and when he descended, he did so slowly, looking across the street. Raincoat man was gone.

A few months later, Taiwan decided that Stinky Bug needed to be killed. He made his move, keeping his plan a secret from Peter. On April 23, 1980, Taiwan sent an assassin to the Kao Wah restaurant to kill David Wong, also known as Stinky Bug, and therefore wound the White Tigers.

What Taiwan didn't know was that Nicky Louie—always the key strategist—was back in New York and had teamed up with Stinky Bug. Nicky figured his odds were better with the small White Tigers than with the Ghost Shadows, who had grown and were loyal to Peter.

Taiwan's plan to kill Stinky Bug failed. Stinky Bug—not knowing that Taiwan was out of hiding, in charge of the Ghost Shadows, and the one who gave the order to take him out— naturally assumed it was Kid Jai who'd tried to kill him. Stinky Bug responded.

The next day, April 24, 1980, the White Tigers sent Irving Woo to kill Kid Jai.

It was about three in the afternoon on Mott Street, the time of day when the street was busiest. Peter was going to join his crew for dinner at Big Wong, the noodle place on Mott, but upon walking in, Peter saw the raincoat man again. This time he was wearing an army jacket, which was strange because it was a warm April night.

As they finished eating, Peter's beeper went off. Peter paid the bill and went outside, scanning for army jacket guy, who was not there. He walked to the bank of pay phones outside the restaurant. Peter made the call to the number on the beeper, hung up, and headed toward Bayard Street. This is when a feeling—like a feather on his neck—occurred. Not a physical feeling, but an instinct, causing Peter to turn around.

As Peter did, he saw the man in the army jacket holding a gun toward him. Peter's first thought was *Clifford Wong*. Peter turned and ran.

The blow from the first bullet hit Peter's head and pushed

him forward. Peter thought that his blood was hot, hotter than he thought it would be. The blow made him tumble down Mott Street. That's when the second bullet hit him in the back.

The Fifth Precinct was the closest city building to Mott Street. Just like Nicky Louie had done the year before, Kid Jai, bleeding from the chest and head, walked into the police station for help. Unlike their response to Nicky Louie, when police officers saw Peter, they sat him in a wooden chair in the lobby and made him look through mug shot books.

"Who shot you?" one cop asked.

"I don't know," Peter lied. "I need to go to the hospital."

"We'll take you once you tell us who shot you." The second cop flipped the book open. "Is it that guy?"

"No."

"How about this one?"

"No."

Peter went through the entire thick book. Then a second one. He was halfway through the third book when a supervisor entered and saw the lobby floor covered with the blood that was still pumping out of Peter.

"If you guys don't get this kid to a hospital, you're not going to have anyone to question," he barked. "Get him out of here and clean up this fucking floor."

Peter was taken to Beekman Hospital, which upset him. Everyone he knew who went to Beekman died; everyone who went to Saint Vincent's had pulled through. Peter wanted to find a clock. That way he would know what time it was when he died.

He found one. It was 4:45 p.m.

That's when I died, Peter thought. *Four forty-five.*

Then he passed out.

Three days later, Peter Chin woke up in the intensive care unit of Beekman Hospital. The first thing he saw was Fu Man

The only photograph of Godfather Nick *(far left corner in the red tie)*, at a wedding of Peter's in-laws while Peter was in prison. *(Author's collection.)*

ft, Ghost Shadow Paul Wong, *:.a.* Whiteface Paul; *rht*, Ghost Shadow George Tom, *:.a.* Lefty, October 1976. *uthor's collection.)*

Mott Street, Chinatown, New York, 1982. *(Gerd Eichmann/Wikimedia Commons.)*

Peter Chin, a.k.a. Kid Jai, 1987,
Federal Correctional Institution,
Terre Haute, Indiana.
(Author's collection.)

Peter Chin, a.k.a. Kid J
twenty-one years c
at JFK Airport, 19
(Author's collectic

Sam, a.k.a. Sasquatch, the Ghost Shadow
who would drag Kenny Wong back to school
at FCI Ray Brook.
(Author's collection.)

Ghost Shadow Shiu Ping (David) Wu,
a.k.a. Applehead, 1977.
(Author's collection.)

e visiting room of the Federal
rrectional Institution, Terre Haute, Indiana.
nter, ten-year-old Anthony Chin;
ght, Robin Chee; *left*, Peter Chin.
bin had brought Anthony to the prison
visit with Anthony's father, Peter.
uthor's collection.)

Robin Chee and his wife and child.
(Author's collection.)

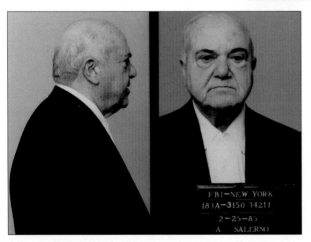

In transit at the Federal Correctional Institution, El Reno, Oklahoma, August 25, 1990. *Top row, left to right*: Steven Yau, a.k.a. Itchy Ass; David Wong, a.k.a. Stinky Bug, founding father of the White Tigers; Shiu Ping Wu, a.k.a. Applehead. *Bottom row, left to right*: Tat, Ghost Shadow associate; Ming, from Thailand, United Bamboo. *(Author's collection.)*

Left, George Tom, a.k.a. Lefty; *right*, Peter Chin, a.k.a. Kid Jai, age sixteen, 1975, standing in front of Kojak's car in Chicago. *(Author's collection.)*

Herbie Sperling, drug kingpin, at the visitors' center at FCI Allenwood, Allenwood, Pennsylvania, where he served with Peter, February 13, 2005. Sperling was one of the first to be sentenced under the continuing criminal enterprise (CCE) statute, or what was called the kingpin charge: life without parole. *(Author's collection.)*

Left, Paul Kwok, a.k.a. Chiu Chow Por, Kung Lok Triad; *right,* Peter Chin, a.k.a. Kid Jai, Federal Correctional Institution, Terre Haute, Indiana, 1988. *(Author's collection.)*

Left, George Tom, a.k.a. Le and two other members of Ghost Shadows, April 19 *(Author's collectic*

Danny Wong, a.k.a. Ah Pai, of the Wah Ching. Danny and Peter were roommates in New York and then Peter traveled to San Francisco to help the Wah Ching take Chinatown back from the Joe Boys. Danny later became the last boss of the Wah Ching, and after his assassination the feds dismantled the group. *(Author's collection.)*

On the far left is George Tom, a.k.a. Lefty; next are Young Goo [as) and Daniel Lee, a.k.a. Monkey; standing with his shirt off is Danny Wong, a.k.a. Ah Pai, of the Wah Ching; the man in the white shirt is unidentified; the man in back is Pipenose; and the last man on the right is Horse Whip (alias), 1970. *(Author's collection.)*

Paul Won, a.k.a. Fu Man, who stayed with Peter in the hospital for three days after he was shot, and Peter Chin. *(Author's collection.)*

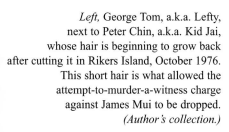

:hony Chin, Peter's son;
. Chin, Peter's mother;
toria, Peter's sister;
' Peter Chin, visitors' center,
eral Correctional Institution,
ersburg, Virginia.
thor's collection.)

Left, George Tom, a.k.a. Lefty, next to Peter Chin, a.k.a. Kid Jai, whose hair is beginning to grow back after cutting it in Rikers Island, October 1976. This short hair is what allowed the attempt-to-murder-a-witness charge against James Mui to be dropped. *(Author's collection.)*

The photo Peter had made in Los Angeles after helping the Wah Ching battle the Joe Boys in San Francisco, when Peter was seventeen. Peter thought it would be funny to look back at this photo when he was an old man. *(Author's collection.)*

Peter Chin *(bottom left)*, Public School after coming to the United Sta at eight years c *(Author's collectic*

Peter today.
(Author's collection.)

sitting next to him, wearing the clothes he'd had on the last time he saw him, three days before.

"You've been here the entire time?" Peter asked.

"We've got guys all over this place," Fu Man reassured him. "At every entrance and all over the building."

Fu Man explained that the gun must have been almost touching Peter's neck when it was fired and the bullet came out of Peter's cheek. He told Peter about the surgery, that Peter's lung had been punctured.

With Peter awake, doctors came in to assess him. Seeing that he was stable, they moved him out of the ICU and into a regular room. Fu Man pushed Peter in a wheelchair, following the nurses to Peter's new room. As the nurses were walking into Peter's new room, as the wheelchair crossed the threshold, the phone next to Peter's new hospital bed rang. Fu Man gave the wheelchair to the nurse and answered it.

"Hello?"

"I want to talk to Kid," the voice on the phone stated.

The nurse pushed Peter toward the phone, and Peter took it.

"Hello?" Peter answered.

"We are still coming for you," the voice said.

What was meant to cause fear, a threatening call from people so connected that they knew the room Peter was assigned to, knew the time he would be rolling into it, had the opposite effect. The man who had spent two unconscious days in intensive care after surgery screamed and cursed.

"You want me?" Kid Jai shouted into the phone, as the nurse rushed to calm him. "Come and get me, motherfucker."

The caller hung up.

Peter spent ten days at Beekman Hospital and then another month recuperating in his Brooklyn home with his wife. There, he allowed the events of the shooting to catch up with him.

"A fraction of an inch," the doctor had said.

In the hospital, the doctor who had operated on Peter

waved the pen he was holding over Peter's X-ray film, which was clipped to the light box. "A fraction to the right, here," the doctor said, pointing with the pen, "and the bullet to your head would have killed you." The doctor pulled down this X-ray and clipped up a new one. "A fraction to the left, here, and this one in your back would have left you paralyzed."

The doctor turned to Peter. "An inch either way would have changed your life, or ended it. You are a very lucky man."

The speech was intended to instill a fear of life on the street. Peter saw it in a different way.

A fraction of an inch, Peter kept thinking. How did he feel about this inch, about these odds?

He didn't feel invincible—people got killed thinking that way—but he did admit that he felt lucky. Lucky was something that you didn't waste. Lucky was something you celebrated.

Peter had known nothing of the world as a child. He didn't see much in his first eight years of life living in a tiny hut with no running water. His one day of school in the New Territory hadn't offered much. After coming to the States, Peter felt that he knew only the twenty square blocks of Chinatown. If this luck was a gift, then he should enjoy this gift and see a little of the world outside of Chinatown. He thought of Danny Mo.

Danny Mo was the head of the Kung Lok Triad in Toronto. Danny had heard of Peter and flew to New York to meet with him. The two had become friends and business partners.

"There's a lot of money to be made in the entertainment business there," Danny said. "I have the connections to bring top-level singers and performers here from Hong Kong."

So Danny, Peter, and Patrick Tse created the company Oriental Arts, an entertainment and promotions company with an office that Danny would run in Toronto, one that Patrick would run in Boston, and one that Peter would run in midtown Manhattan on Twenty-Third Street. The company was doing well.

In Canada, guns were incredibly hard to find, so one time when Peter and his crew drove up to see Mo in Toronto, Peter brought Mo a surprise.

"I have something for you." Peter smiled after they had greeted each other. Peter opened the hood and fished around the side to a hidden area. He pulled out a German-made machine gun and what they called "brother and sister" guns, two new .38 revolvers, still in the box.

"You know," Mo said, holding the guns in wonder, "I might be the first Triad member in all of Canada to own a machine gun."

When Peter came up with the idea of going back to Hong Kong, he couldn't get Danny Mo out of his head, so he called him.

"Yeah, I'll go," Danny said without hesitation. "I have a lot of people I want you to meet in Hong Kong, and it could help the business."

Peter began to plan for his first real trip. First, he needed to visit Mongo.

Peter went to the Chesapeake Detention Facility in Baltimore and sat with Mongo in the visiting room. Mongo listened to Peter describe all that was happening within the Ghost Shadows. "It sounds to me"—Mongo looked around to make sure listening ears weren't close—"that Taiwan needs to go. You have my permission, if you need it, to take care of him."

"No." Peter shook his head. "He's your childhood friend, and I'm working on getting you out of here. When you're out and can look at both sides for yourself, if you want to do it then," Peter said, "then I'll take care of it."

Peter left the prison and drove home, thinking about his upcoming flight.

Throughout the 1970s, the population of Hong Kong grew at an incredible rate. The city's economy exploded with the manufacturing business. Hong Kong's government expanded to meet these demands but was unable to respond fast enough for the population's growing need for services. This allowed the already strong Triad organized crime presence to become even stronger.

Tea money, black money, or *hell money* were the terms for any payoff, bribe, or extortion. This practice was not only accepted in Hong Kong but was expected, the way of life.

An ambulance driver could quote the *hell money* needed before allowing an injured person in an ambulance. Teachers had prices of *black money* to increase students' grades or for special treatment. Hospitals expected tips for bringing medication or even getting sick people registered.

The most concentrated section of corruption was in the police department. Police officers not only expected *tea money* for regular services, such as responding to a citizen's call, but were also paid to look the other way to protect drug activities, gambling, and other crimes.

In 1974, the Independent Commission Against Corruption (ICAC) was formed in Hong Kong specifically to go after corruption in law enforcement.

ICAC caused a mass exodus of corrupt police officers from Hong Kong, where these officials grabbed the money they had collected illegally—in some cases, tens of millions of dollars—and fled to the more forgiving Chinatowns of New York, Boston, and San Francisco. The police chief of Hong Kong, Peter Godber, escaped prosecution by fleeing the country.

Tse Chiu Chan, who went by the name Eddie Chan, was a former Hong Kong police sergeant who fled corruption charges and immigrated to New York in 1975, where he opened his funeral home and restaurants. He had ties to the Kung Lok Triad and was better known by his street name, the Sixth Dragon.

When Eddie Chan arrived in New York, he found a Chinatown under the tight control of Uncle Benny, who ruled from his seat at the Hip Sing Tong. Eddie Chan realized that Uncle

Benny was too powerful to challenge directly, so he joined the rival On Leong Tong.

Eddie put his money to work creating his public image in New York by becoming the chairman of the National Chinese Welfare Council, where he worked with members of the US Congress to help Chinese immigrants and nationals. He sat as the vice chair of the United Orient Bank, and he personally owned a funeral parlor, jewelry store, antique store, several restaurants, and movie theaters in New York's Chinatown.

In Hong Kong, everyone from the newest rookie cop to the heads of the departments were on the take. If you were that one honest cop who didn't take bribes, and if a few beatings didn't change your mind, you simply disappeared. Eddie Chan had enjoyed a very successful reign in Hong Kong police bribery, and he came to New York's Chinatown with several million dollars in tow.

Uncle Benny was fighting a bribery case that, if convicted, could imprison him for six years. With Uncle Benny gone, this would create a power vacuum that Eddie Chan was preparing to fill.

In the Hong Kong that Peter and Danny Mo were stepping into in 1981, the corruption may have been pulled from the police department; however, it was still incredibly strong in one profitable sector of the Hong Kong economy: entertainment.

Every facet of entertainment was controlled by the Triads, from permits to casting and booking to catering. It was no surprise that when Danny began introducing Peter to people, they were a solid mixture of Triad leaders and movie stars— and sometimes, Triad leaders who *were* movie stars.

The opulence of Hong Kong shocked Peter, with nightclubs that were so large they had full-sized top-of-the-line Rolls-Royce cars inside the actual clubs to drive you to different sections of the building.

Peter Chin and Danny Mo spent four months traveling through Hong Kong and Taiwan, meeting with some of the cities' most prominent movie stars and Triad members. By the time Peter left, he had made several powerful new friends and established relationships with profitable entertainment businesses.

In 1982, Uncle Benny lost his last appeal and was sentenced to a six-year sentence in Lewisburg Federal Penitentiary. Eddie Chan stepped in and filled the power void Uncle Benny left behind. Soon, Eddie Chan was the face and fist of the On Leong Tong, which became more powerful than Uncle Benny's Hip Sing. In 1982, Eddie Chan sent a messenger to Kid Jai. Eddie Chan needed a favor.

At that time, Patrick Tse was about as big a Hong Kong movie star as you could get. He was performing at the Tropicana in Atlantic City, and the Flying Dragons saw this as an opportunity. Ten Flying Dragons took over the VIP suite where Patrick and his wife were and held them for ransom.

Kid Jai's new friendships with the top level of Hong Kong entertainment made him the most likely person to reach out to in situations like this one.

"Can you go to Atlantic City and fix this?" Eddie Chan's messenger asked. "We can have a helicopter take you, or a limo."

Peter didn't like the idea of flying in a helicopter, so he said that the limo was fine. Soon, he and two other Ghost Shadows headed to Atlantic City.

When they arrived at the VIP suite at the Tropicana, it was a tense few minutes at the door. Peter knocked. There was a pause.

"Who is it?" came the voice.

"It's Kid Jai."

There was some rumbling, a pause, and then the door opened. Peter and the Ghost Shadows walked in.

Inside the luxury suite was a very nervous Patrick Tse and

his wife, along with ten Flying Dragons. Peter scanned the crowd and saw a face he recognized, Norman Luk, also known as Long-necked Giraffe. He asked to speak to Norman privately.

"I want to give you face," Peter said. "And I'm hoping you will do the same for me. Patrick is a friend of mine, and I came all the way from New York to resolve this. I'm hoping we can."

The message was clear and received. Here was a way out of this situation without violence. The Flying Dragons left.

Peter and Patrick spent some time chatting about the mutual friends they had in Hong Kong, and then Peter left, too.

Alan Tang was that rare breed that was both a top-ranking box office movie star and an active Triad member. In 1981, Alan Tang was one of the biggest box office draws. He got to know Peter when Peter and Danny Mo were in Hong Kong setting things up for Oriental Arts.

Peter had met Alan on several of his and Mo's trips to Hong Kong. On one trip, they waited for Alan at their hotel.

"What time is Alan picking us up?" Peter asked Mo.

At about ten thirty, Peter turned on the TV. He saw a live TV broadcast with Alan on it.

"Hey." Peter laughed. "If this is live, that's why Alan isn't here. He's there."

"Son of a bitch." Mo picked up the phone and called one of the Triad leaders to complain about Alan being late. Twenty minutes later, still wearing the same clothes from the interview, Alan rushed into the hotel room to pick up Peter and Mo.

In 1982, Mo set up a meeting with Alan and Peter in New York.

"People in Hong Kong are dying for a movie like this," Alan told Peter. "People want to know about New York's Chinatown, about gangsters, but most of them will never get the chance to come here. We want to film it right here."

Peter listened to the story and had one condition. "Don't make the Ghost Shadows look bad in this movie," Peter said. "That's all I ask."

They agreed that the two rival gangs in the film would represent the Ghost Shadows and the Flying Dragons, but they would use different names and stay respectful. Alan offered Peter a piece of the net profits.

"No," Peter said. "If you promise not to make us look bad, I'll help you from my heart. I have other people to answer to about how we look in this." Alan agreed.

Permits were pushed through, payoffs were made, and soon the project was greenlit. The film was ready for production, but the biggest hurdle was getting generators. Film production takes a great deal of power, and huge industrial generators are needed on film sets. With the New York construction boom of the 1980s, generators were hard to come by. Peter talked to all the businesses owners in Chinatown and asked for the favor of running extension cords out of their shops and restaurants so the production crew could plug in.

New York's Chinatown provided free power, one shop at a time, to the production of *New York Chinatown,* an action film about two fictitious warring organized crime factions in New York's Chinatown that supposedly represented the Ghost Shadows and the Flying Dragons.

In 1982, Peter decided to fulfill the promise he had made to himself while delivering laundry for his sister almost ten years before. Peter had been in many limousines since then, but he'd never had one available to him at all times. He hired a limousine and driver to be available twenty-four hours a day for three months. When negotiating this deal with the limousine company, the company informed Peter that for the price he would pay for a driver and car, he could buy the limousine. Peter didn't care. The deal was made, and the limo and driver were parked on Mott Street for three months, night and day.

Peter used it mostly to take his three-year-old son, Anthony, to the park, and sometimes he just sat in the back, allowing the fact to settle that he had fulfilled his dream and his promise.

Long-term residents of Chinatown still remember seeing a limousine parked on Mott Street for three months in the summer of 1982. Many sat and rode in it as children when the driver had nothing to do.

With the limousine at the ready, Oriental Arts was doing well promoting Chinese musical artists. It organized the artists and venues and promoted huge shows for the Chinese communities in San Francisco, Boston, Toronto, and New York.

Lisa Wang was the darling of the Chinese community. Born in Shanghai, she was an actress on Chinese television and sang with the Cantonese Opera and the Four Golden Flowers. Peter and Mo financed her US tour, which was going very well.

Mo loved this part of the business. Peter, not so much. Although somewhat profitable, the work was tedious and long. There were flights to arrange, venues to book, unions to deal with. There was always the difficult aspect of giving everyone in Chinatown the correct face. When shows came to New York, such as Lisa Wang's, Peter needed to give front-row tickets to the tongs. Which tong do you have on which night? Who gets opening night? You definitely couldn't sit them together.

There were all the demands from the performers.

When Lisa Wang finished the Boston leg of her tour, she came to New York. She required four bodyguards to travel first-class with her. She needed a makeup artist and a hair stylist on twenty-four-hour call, and, when the curtain opened, she wanted the flag to rise in a specific way and a conveyor to carry her onto the stage to the microphone. She also needed the stage built exactly to a specific shape and size.

When Peter contracted out the construction of that stage, the contractors found it impossible to do. Even by taking out the first three rows, they could not make the stage the size and shape Lisa wanted. She refused to come. Tickets had been sold, venues had been rented; this was not about money, this was about face. Canceling was disrespectful to Peter and the Ghost Shadows. Peter got on the phone with Patrick Tse.

"If she isn't coming to New York," Peter said, "then she isn't going back to Hong Kong." He paused so Tse understood his meaning. "If Lisa decides to go back to Hong Kong anyway, I will have people waiting to bring her to me."

The message was passed on to Lisa Wang. She and her four bodyguards were on the next flight to New York.

There were unofficial *uniforms* on the streets of Chinatown. Civilians, those everyday people, would always look like what they are: regular people on their way to work in a shop, factory, or office. Street guys were always recognizable by the way they dressed and how they carried themselves. If a Mob guy were to venture down from Little Italy for some dumplings, he would easily be recognized by his suit or bowling shirt. One of the most common uniform on the streets of Chinatown was the one worn by waiters. Black pants, white button-down shirts. They always looked tired because they worked all the time and were always hurrying—either on their way to work or heading for a few hours of sleep after. They were everywhere.

With all of the waiters on Mott Street that day, it's not clear how Peter spotted him, but he did. This waiter walked by, and Peter took a second for his face to register, then he turned and called back.

"Colgate?"

Colgate turned, took a second to register as well, then smiled. "Peter?"

Colgate had brought the bowl of rice for Peter when he was thirteen and living on the streets, eight years before. They hadn't seen each other since, and the two old friends caught up.

Peter learned that Colgate was married with two children. Colgate and some partners were saving up to buy a small restaurant, but the financing was becoming difficult, so Colgate was still a waiter.

Peter smiled and prodded, asking what restaurant Colgate was looking to buy, where it was, and how much they were asking. The two old friends parted ways, but not without Peter getting Colgate's phone number first.

Peter climbed the stairs to the Ghost Shadows' apartment and wrote down all the information Colgate had given him.

"Here." Peter handed the paper to a Ghost Shadow. "Go buy this place. I don't care what it costs, just get it."

A week later, Peter called and asked Colgate to come visit him. When he arrived, Peter gave him a thick manila envelope. Inside were the papers Colgate needed to sign to buy the restaurant and the $40,000 to do it.

Colgate looked at the paperwork and the money. When he lifted his head, he was crying. Before Colgate could speak, Peter did.

"I was drowning." Peter was crying, too. "You threw me a life jacket. It was only a bowl of rice to you," he said, "but I never, ever forgot it."

Peter turned away, embarrassed that he was crying. "I told you I would make it up to you someday."

In the early 1980s, the heroin trafficking business in the United States was exploding, and along with it another illegal but lesser-known industry that organized crime in Chinatown was beginning to get involved in. Not as gritty as heroin, not as brash or flashy, but every bit as profitable, and all controlled by the Wah Ching.

Chinese videotape rentals.

The videotape revolution had begun. Low-cost videocassette recorders created a huge need for videotapes, and there was an enormous profit to be made by those who could provide these videotapes for rent. The cost to the consumer of buying the tapes was high—sometimes $100 or so—but you could rent these same tapes for $2 or less. The convenience of not having to work around TV and theater schedules was difficult to compete with.

In 1985, the global videotape rental industry was worth more than $3 billion—again, just in VHS rentals—and it wouldn't reach its peak until 1990, when it topped $8 billion.

In 1982, VHS rental was at the very beginning of this boom across the country. In Chinatown communities, this boom was intensified. Before, residents had to rely on local Chinese theaters for their favorite films from China. In Hong Kong, there were only two TV channels that produced content, but these were not easily accessed in the United States. The American Chinese public was dying to see these series, soap operas, TV shows, and movies they'd been missing.

Videotape rentals made that possible, and now American Chinatowns could access these once-hard-to-find films, TV shows, soap operas, sports, all in their native language, and watch them on their own schedules. If you knew where to go to get them, the choices were endless. Chinese theaters quickly felt the pinch and many closed, unable to draw in the crowds they once had.

Vincent Jew of the Los Angeles Wah Ching saw this opportunity and decided to mix the legitimate with the illegitimate. He wanted to take the legal franchise video rights, a legitimate business, extort it, then use his reputation with the Wah Ching and use legal protection when needed. First, he needed to get those rights, which would require all the Wah Ching muscle. Vincent Jew strong-armed the people he needed and was given those exclusive rights.

Since Peter had left San Francisco to try to help the Wah Ching five years before, they had built their power back up over the Joe Boys and now controlled most of San Francisco's Chinatown. Vincent Jew and Sweet Plum had risen in rank and were a big part of the Wah Ching, as well as being kingpins in the Chinese videotape industry.

Chinese videotape stores were popping up all over. Franchise fees controlled by the Wah Ching were extremely expensive, as were the tapes themselves, which required owners to purchase from them directly. Since the Wah Ching were on the West Coast, there were many East Coast gangs who decided it was worth the risk to try to bypass these fees and make illegal copies of Chinese tapes to rent out.

To better understand Peter Chin, it's important to mention how little grudges meant to him. Peter never took the past seriously, and he forgave easily, even those people who tried to kill him. When Stinky Bug asked to resolve the differences between himself and Peter, Kid Jai had no issue meeting with him and forgiving him. Soon, they were back on good terms.

Stinky Bug not only saw an opportunity in videotape rentals but also an advantage in them, given Peter's reputation and connection with the Wah Ching.

"They won't fuck with you," Stinky Bug said. "You be the upfront man, we'll say it's your store, we'll do all the work and cut you in."

"I'll do it." Peter put his hand on the shoulder of his old friend. "But don't cut me in. I'll do it as a favor to you."

Stinky Bug went to work. He set up a small production studio with banks of VCRs and began illegally mass-producing Chinese videotapes. Soon, they had enough to open their store on Bayard Street. Business was booming.

Word got back to the Wah Ching that New York was opening video stores without paying them the franchise fees or buying product from them. Armed with the legal business side, mixed in with Wah Ching muscle, they conducted a raid in New York to shut down these stores. Within days, every illegal Chinese videotape rental store in New York City was shut down and locked up, and the owners were facing felony pirating charges. Every store but one. Peter's store on Bayard Street. His was one store that was purposely left out of the raid. Even the Wah Ching wouldn't mess with that store.

There were many franchised stores, and the corporate store opened next to Peter Wong's old nightclub. Vincent Jew and the Wah Ching never sought Peter's permission or blessing to open. But this store was also their New York headquarters. This was a serious sign of disrespect.

Sweet Plum of the Wah Ching requested a sit-down with Kid Jai regarding Peter's store. Peter agreed and the two met and were soon discussing an offer the Wah Ching wanted to make Peter: the Wah Ching would waive the $50,000 franchising fee and lower the cost of each videotape down to $35 a tape.

Peter thought about how Stinky Bug could rent one tape and turn it into twenty for less than $35. More importantly, he thought about the disrespect the Wah Ching had shown by opening that store in New York in secret, without going through the Ghost Shadows.

Peter listened, then stood up. "That won't work for me." He shook Sweet Plum's hand. "It was good to see you again."

Sweet Plum had been dismissed.

A few weeks later, Vincent Jew asked for a sit-down with Peter. They met in a French restaurant in Manhattan. Vincent started the conversation with some flattery about how Peter had risen since he'd last seen him as a fifteen-year-old kid in San Francisco. Peter listened to the comments and waited for Vincent to mention the store the Wah Ching had opened. He didn't. What Vincent did was repeat the offer Sweet Plum had given Peter, with only slightly better terms.

You are West Coast, Peter thought. *I am East Coast. You come here and think you don't need to show me respect? You don't ask permission to operate in my territory, you just do it?*

In a respectful way, Peter told Vincent that this deal wouldn't work for him. Vincent Jew was dismissed as well.

At the time, there was the Wah Ching corporate store and the stores that paid the franchise fees. But Peter's store was the only bootleg one not paying a fee.

*   *   *

True to his word, Peter looked after Peter Wong's family after Peter's death over the shark fin incident. Shortly after Peter Wong's death, a playboy type from the Hip Sing thought it was a good time to move in on Peter Wong's widow. Peter had a Ghost Shadow stationed outside of her house for several weeks. The playboy lost interest.

Peter Wong's son, Kenny, required a little more attention. Like many poor Asian kids, Kenny was drawn to the streets of Chinatown. He was skipping school and was seen at the arcades or on the street corners around Mott and Pell Streets. Peter had the Ghost Shadows constantly looking for Kenny Wong.

"If you see him," Peter said, "drag his ass back to school."

This didn't deter Kenny, only increased his vigilance. "Let me know if you see any of my uncle's guys—Kid Jai's guys," Kenny said to his friends while throwing another quarter into a Pac-Man machine.

Kenny was on Ghost Shadow turf, so it wasn't easy to hide, and he was always seen and dragged back to school. Over time, Kenny was more and more brazen with each Ghost Shadow that took him back to school, with the exception of one: Sasquatch. Sasquatch was an intimidating presence, and when he dragged Kenny back to school, Kenny usually stayed, partly because Kenny knew that Sasquatch would be waiting at the back entrance—Kenny's secret escape route. Facing the big man twice was not a wise move.

Pablo Escobar was to cocaine what Limpy Ho was to heroin. Pablo controlled the world cocaine market from Colombia, and Limpy controlled the world heroin market from Hong Kong. When one of Limpy's capos asked to sit down with Peter in New York, Peter had a good idea what the subject of the conversation would be.

"We want to give you five hundred pounds," the capo said. "You pay us for two hundred and fifty pounds and keep the rest. Don't worry about getting it into the country, we have that covered. We'll keep delivering to you and you pay us half each time."

Peter did the math. At two hundred and fifty pounds at the current wholesale value for heroin, his cut alone would be $25 million, just for this first delivery.

It was tempting, very, but drugs and counterfeiting were two areas Peter wanted to keep the Ghost Shadows out of. In the past, when the Ghost Shadows had had the opportunity to buy some stolen plates for US bills, Peter didn't even want to see them. The risks were way too high. Peter felt the same way about drugs and didn't want the Ghost Shadows involved, no matter the profit.

"I'm honored you thought of me." Peter weighed every word. "And I don't mean any disrespect, but this isn't for me. I know there are many here who will be grateful to take your offer."

Peter knew that the next organization the capo would approach would be the Flying Dragons. But Peter also knew that the Scientist, the Dai Lo, would be opposed to it. Then they would keep going until they found those that weren't.

The man Peter called Uncle Tang, from the restaurant where Peter got the tea and cakes for the factory teatime when he was helping his mother as a child, was in trouble. A member of Uncle Tang's family had been diagnosed with cancer and needed $5,000 for treatment. Uncle Tang was a good, solid man and had no knowledge of the tongs or where to go to get a loan of this size. All he knew was that a traditional bank wouldn't give him one. He reached out to the only person he could think of who might help: Bark Chin, a.k.a. the Cow. After all, the Cow was a member of the Hip Sing Tong.

Uncle Tang went to the Chin apartment on East Broadway to meet with the Cow, who listened.

"I cannot help you," the Cow said, hinting that he had the power to help but had decided not to. "But I know someone who can. Go see my son."

Uncle Tang did. When he went to the Golden Taipei to meet with Peter, Uncle told him what the Cow had said. Peter immediately understood that his father had set this up so the Cow didn't need to do anything to help but would gain respect just for providing the pathway to his son.

Peter listened to the story. "Uncle Tang," he said with a smile. "I will help you. You don't need to pay me back—it's a gift because you have always been kind to me. If you choose to pay me back, this is what I ask: I'd like you to go back to my father, at night when my mother is home, and tell my father that I was able to help you, but I did it out of the kindness you showed me as a child and it had nothing to do with my father at all. Tell him that I said that my father has no influence over me, or over Chinatown."

Uncle Tang agreed. Peter gave him the money and, being an honorable man, Uncle went back to East Broadway. With Kiu in the other room listening, Uncle Tang gave the message to Peter's father.

Peter Chin discovered that pretending to kill someone could be the best way to save their lives.

Kojak was the president of the On Leong Tong in Chicago, a big shot. Unlike other big shots in the Chinatown underworld, Kojak was friendly and spent time with everyone. He was completely down to earth. Kojak was kind to Peter when Peter was coming up, and they remained close as Peter climbed the ladder. Every time Kojak came to New York to meet with the On Leong, he reached out to Peter and they would stay out all night. Unlike other big shots in Chinese organized crime, Kojak wasn't a gambler, but he did love to drink; he was able to down two bottles of whiskey a night and still hold a conversation by the end.

One day, Eddie Chan summoned Peter to his office. Eddie had been slowly forming the New York chapter of the On Leong and having business flow through New York. At the same time, Kojak lost his bid as On Leong president, so Eddie wanted to hit Kojak while he was weakest so that he didn't become a threat.

Peter met with Eddie Chan. When he heard Kojak's name, he listened intently.

"Kojak has to go," Eddie Chan said. "I'd like you to go to Chicago and take care of him."

Peter thought for a moment. "Sure, I can do that."

Peter received his instructions and left, but he had no intention of hurting Kojak. He knew that pretending to be the hit man was the best way to save him. Peter took Potato and another Ghost Shadow and headed to Chicago. There, they met with the sitting On Leong president, who gave Peter six guns to use to kill Kojak.

"Six guns for one guy?" Peter asked.

"Eddie wants to make sure you have everything you need." Peter took the weapons and the three headed out. He stopped at a phone booth to set up a meeting with Kojak.

In a Mob movie, this would be the perfect double-cross setup for a hit. You warn a guy that he is going to be killed, that you are the one sent to kill him, but you have no intention of doing so and are his friend, loyal to him. You meet with him only to kill him anyway. The ways of Chinatown are different. Peter Chin met up with Kojak at a bar outside of Chicago's Chinatown but didn't tell him why he wanted to meet.

When Peter told Kojak that Eddie Chan had sent him to kill him, Kojak was shocked. "You take off for a few weeks," Peter said. "I'll be seen looking for you. I'll make all the right connections, go through all the places, but you'll be gone, and I won't be able to find you."

"I have some things to do in Wisconsin," Kojak said. "I can go there."

"Great. Do that."

Kojak did. For two days, Peter and the three Ghost Shadows were seen all around Chinatown in Chicago making inquiries, asking questions, pretending to look for Kojak. This continued until one day, when Peter heard squealing tires and an unmarked police car pulled up on the sidewalk in front of him. Two detectives got out, guns pointed at Peter and his men.

"Kid Jai!" they screamed. "Hands behind your head; face that wall."

Peter and his men complied.

The detectives patted down the Ghost Shadows. Since the group had no plans to kill Kojak, the six guns weren't on them but safely hidden at the hotel. The grilling began.

"Why are you in Chicago?" the first detective asked.

"Visiting," Peter responded.

"Visiting who?" the second barked.

"A friend."

"What friend?"

The questions continued, short answers were given, and it was clear it was going nowhere. The detectives ended the confrontation with a warning: "We know how long you've been in Chicago. We know where you've been, we know what flight you came in on, and even what fucking Holiday Inn you're staying at. If anything goes down while you're here, we will pin it on you."

When the detectives got back in their car, Peter realized that this encounter was exactly what they needed. A perfect reason to stop hunting for Kojak. They couldn't kill Kojak now—there was too much heat. As Peter planned their trip back home, something gnawed at him. How did the Chicago detectives know so much about him, down to the very hotel they were staying at? Peter Chin filed this away as excellent police work, but that was only because Peter Chin didn't yet know about the informant within the Ghost Shadows. He didn't know about *Casper.*

Peter and his group went back to the hotel to get their things, as well as the guns. Since Peter wouldn't be able to take six guns on the plane back to New York, they took an Amtrak back.

Days later, after a slow train ride, Peter was summoned to see Eddie Chan. Peter explained what happened, that the police knew Peter was there, that anything would have been pinned on him, that he couldn't leave the guns, so he brought them back to New York.

Kojak lived for another three years.

Dice was excited. "Wait till you see it," he said, leading Peter out of the Golden Taipei.

Outside was a new 1982 Mercedes-Benz 380. Dice beamed as he walked Peter around the new car.

"What do you think?" Dice opened up the driver's-side door. "Look, it has automatic seat belts; you don't even have to put them on yourself."

Peter looked at the car and then back at Dice. How could this man who was so much older than him be so stupid? Dice had no legitimate businesses to claim where the income to purchase the car had come from. Everything he had now was his newfound drug wealth.

"What's wrong with you?" Peter asked.

"What, you don't like it?"

"You're not a stockbroker or a lawyer, you're a heroin dealer. Why are you driving around in this with no way to explain it?"

Dice brushed this off, showing Peter the power seats.

Peter Chin was spending money as well; however, he had legitimate businesses to explain things. With disposable income more available now than ever before, Peter became very interested in horse racing. He and Fu Man went early in the morning to Belmont Park, Aqueduct, or Saratoga to bet on the horses. During these trips they got to know a wealthy man named Andrew who owned a racehorse, and they all became friends. In a strange sort of coincidental connection, Andrew had a business partner who was connected to the garment district in Chinatown. This woman was dating a cop, and this cop's job was to translate the Ghost Shadows surveillance tapes from Chinese to English. And this cop loved to talk about work with his girlfriend.

"The cops have a guy inside," Andrew told Peter as they walked through the stables.

"My inside?" Peter shook his head. "Impossible."

"They threatened him with a year and half in prison unless he cooperated, so he did."

"A year and a half?" Peter laughed. "He broke for that?" A man who betrayed everyone for a year and a half had no honor.

"He's wearing a wire and they even have a code name for this operation," Andrew insisted. "They call it Operation Casper."

Peter understood the connection between Casper the Friendly Ghost and the Ghost Shadows.

"I do know the guy's last name," Andrew said. "It's Wong."

Wong was a very common Chinese name. Peter had five guys in the Ghost Shadows with the last name Wong. He wondered about all of them.

It didn't surprise Peter that law enforcement had informants. Peter knew that Detective Neil Mauriello from the Jade Squad had an informant with the street name Long Man inside the Flying Dragons. Long Man had the bad luck of allowing the recording device to actually fall from his shirt during a Flying Dragon meeting. They found Long Man's body in a burning car near the New Jersey Turnpike.

Which Wong was Casper?

On July 15, 1982, Peter and his wife, Ida, went to the Golden Dragon restaurant at 59 Mott Street. The place was busy, and

Peter, with his street sense and habit of scanning a room as soon as he entered it, picked up two interesting things. The first was that there were other Ghost Shadows there—about six of them, newer guys, including a kid named Sammy. Peter acknowledged the table, and they did the same back.

The second was that there was a white woman sitting at the bar alone. Caucasians were the minority in Chinatown, but other than Godfather Nick, they usually traveled in groups. This woman not only was alone but looked completely out of place.

Peter turned to Ida. "See that woman at the bar?" he said. "She looks—"

But before Peter could finish, Ida did it for him. "Sad."

The waiter arrived, Peter and Ida ordered, and Peter had a round of drinks sent over to the table of Ghost Shadows as well as to the sad woman at the bar.

Peter and Ida ate and left. Eight hours later, when Peter and Ida were back in their Brooklyn home, that sad woman, twenty-one-year-old Rita Nixon from Portsmouth, Virginia, was raped, strangled with an electrical cord, and left dead in an alley off Catherine Street by the same group of Ghost Shadows who were sitting at that table at the Golden Dragon.

When the news of what happened to Rita Nixon reached Peter, he was furious. Having to kill enemies of the Ghost Shadows to protect the family was part of the deal. This was pointless and cruel. Peter still felt guilty about the two innocent men who were killed because a few Flying Dragons were convinced the men were White Tigers, but this? This was too much.

When the Ghost Shadows were arrested for the rape and murder of Rita Nixon, for which there was an overwhelming amount of evidence, the normal route was for the Dai Lo to provide legal support and bail if possible.

"They'll need some help," Raymond, Peter's driver, stated.

"They'll need lawyers and if the lawyers can arrange it, they'll need bail money and to be bailed out. If you want I can—"

"Let them rot," Peter told Raymond.

"Huh?"

"I won't do anything to help them," Peter said. "Nothing."

"But they're our guys," Raymond said, sounding surprised.

"Not anymore."

Peter's words were recorded on the wire that Peter's driver, Raymond Wong, code-named Casper, was wearing. It was given to Nancy Ryan and her team of state prosecutors, who were building their case against Peter Chin and the Ghost Shadows. Since Peter had seen the men accused of this crime at the Golden Dragon the same day Rita Nixon was raped and killed, they were hoping to find a way to implicate Kid Jai in this. His wasn't the kind of response they were hoping for.

Peter knew he had to determine who the informer within the Ghost Shadows was. With five Wongs to choose from, he wasn't sure. He had eliminated three of them as suspects, but he had to be sure.

Peter brought all five men with the last name Wong together.

"There's an informer here," he said. "Working for the police. His last name is Wong. Who is it?"

Peter watched their reactions. Gauged the responses. Judged the body language.

It's Raymond, Peter knew right away. The meeting ended and over the next week this guess was confirmed. Raymond Wong never came back.

With the informer gone, police pressure increased on the Ghost Shadows and Peter Chin. In 1981, Andrew, his girlfriend Doris, Peter, and his wife Ida flew to Toronto to visit Danny Mo. Mo picked them up and on the foggy drive from the airport, it happened. They were stopped at a right light on Spadina Avenue. Suddenly, the car was surrounded by Royal Canadian Mounted Police.

"Kid Jai!" the shout echoed. Armed policemen pointed guns at Mo and Peter. "Freeze."

They were taken into the precinct for questioning.

The first thing Peter noticed was that the Toronto Police Station was not only the nicest police station he had ever been in but one of the nicest buildings he had ever been in. It had a glass dome. It was clean and open and very modern, like a conference center or the set of a game show. When they put Peter and Mo in the lineup, it was on an actual stage, like the ones for beauty pageants. If you took a photo of the Fifth Precinct in New York and told an architect to build the exact opposite, this would be the result.

Peter and Mo were separated and questioned.

"What are you doing in Canada, Kid Jai?" the officer asked.

"Visiting my friend," he answered.

They started placing photographs on the table. Photos of Andrew, Doris, himself, and Ida leaving the plane. Peter couldn't believe they had so many photos so quickly.

"RCMP has been tracking you the minute you stepped on Canadian soil."

"Then you know we haven't done anything," Peter said.

"We can book you for prostitution right now," the officer said. "Both of you brought prostitutes across a national border. That would be trafficking, too."

Peter laughed. He couldn't wait to tell Ida that they were calling her a prostitute. He knew that if this was all they had, they were reaching.

The interrogation went on for hours and the authorities learned nothing. They were all released with a warning.

"We know you're here," the officer said. "So if anything happens in Canada, anywhere, we are going to pin it on you."

They all got on the plane and flew back to New York.

The same thing happened to Mo when he flew to Hong Kong. When Peter heard that Mo had a five-hour layover in New York, he didn't want Mo to be stuck in an airport.

"You don't want to stay in an airport for five hours," Peter insisted. "I'll pick you up. We'll go get something to eat and get a massage."

Peter picked Mo up from the airport, they ate, they got a massage, Peter drove him back to the airport, and Mo flew to Hong Kong.

When Mo arrived, he called Peter.

"Kid," he said, "I hadn't even left the airport and the feds were all over me. Picking me up and grilling me about what we did during those five hours in New York."

They had not taken Mo to a police station this time but to the ICAC, internal affairs. To the most serious floor they had, the fifth floor. The federal and international pressure on Kid Jai and the Ghost Shadows was very high and was increasing.

At the same time, things between David Wong, a.k.a. Stinky Bug, and Peter weren't great, but they were improving. They'd had a few phone calls and tensions were low enough for Stinky Bug to ask for a favor.

"He wants to come back," Stinky Bug said over the phone. "To New York. He's in hiding."

"Who?" Peter asked

"Irving," Stinky Bug answered. Peter knew that Irving Woo was Raincoat Guy, the man who had shot Peter in the head and back.

Peter Chin had some faults, but holding on to grudges was never one of them. In his life he's forgiven everyone with the exception of his father. Peter could never forgive his father for the pain he caused his mother and sisters, but forgive the man who shot him twice and missed killing him or paralyzing him by an inch? Yeah, he could do that.

"I won't touch him," Peter said. "He can come back."

"He'll need to hear that from you."

They set up a meeting at the new Grand Hyatt hotel in Manhattan. They met at the coffee shop, which was public and was a neutral place for Irving to feel safe. Peter arrived. Irving did a few minutes later. The custom was for Irving to serve Peter his tea, a sign of asking forgiveness. If Peter accepted the tea, then the forgiveness was granted. Irving poured the tea, but his hands were shaking so badly most of the tea spilled from the cup. When the cup was half full, Irving held the cup out to Peter. The cup was shaking so badly that Peter thought there wouldn't be any tea left.

Peter took the cup, nodded, and sipped the small amount of tea that still remained.

Irving Woo was forgiven and allowed to come back to New York to rejoin the White Tigers.

Sparerib was released from prison when Peter was recovering from being shot by Irving Woo. Sparerib spent his time with Robert Hu, a.k.a. Taiwanese Boy, listening to his mistrust and fear of Peter. Sparerib never visited Peter at his home after the shooting, and then Peter was gone for four months with Danny Mo in Hong Kong and Taiwan. During this time, Sparerib began to see Taiwanese Boy's way of thinking.

It was later revealed in the court documents of Nicky Louie's plea agreement that Taiwan, Nicky Louie, and Sparerib were planning to assassinate Peter Chin because they felt that Peter would soon come after them.

This is when Sparerib began wearing a bulletproof vest. Peter did not know this, nor did he have any plans to kill Taiwanese Boy or Sparerib; however, he was still keeping an eye out for Nicky. He was not seeking out Nicky, but because Nicky still posed a threat, Peter was ready to respond at a moment's notice.

One snowy night a year before, Peter pulled his new Lincoln Mark IV onto Mott Street.

"Wow," Applehead said. "Let me take it for a spin."

Soon, Peter was in the passenger seat and Applehead was driving around Chinatown.

"This is nice," Applehead said. "Does it have—"

He never finished his sentence because Peter saw Nicky Louie driving the other direction. "Hey!" Peter yelled. "That's Nicky. Turn around."

Applehead was able to get the boat of a car turned around, and soon they caught up with Nicky. The new Lincoln had a moonroof, so Peter popped out of it with his pistol. When they were close enough, Peter fired at Nicky's car. Three bullets hit the car, but because of Peter's bad aim, none came close to Nicky. Nicky took a side street and headed down by the Southern District Court, heading uptown, and they lost him.

On February 14, 1981, John Chan, a.k.a. Sparerib, was at the Music Palace theater at 93 Bowery, which was Flying Dragons territory. He was followed in by two Flying Dragons, who waited for everyone to be seated. When the kung fu film began, one of the Flying Dragons crept to where Sparerib was sitting and fired a pistol into the back of Sparerib's head, killing the twenty-two-year-old instantly.

Sparerib was wearing his bulletproof vest.

Although Detective Neil Mauriello of the Jade Squad had a certain rapport with the organized crime groups of Chinatown, his partner, Phil Agosta, was different, more direct.

Phil approached Peter on Mott Street. "I need to talk to you."

"I've got nothing to talk about," Peter responded.

"Oh, I think you do." Phil handed Peter his business card. "I think you'll want to hear what I have to say."

They made plans to meet at six that night at the World Trade Center coffee shop. Peter was curious, so he went, but he brought a guy with him. He and Phil sat down, and a Ghost Shadow guarded the door.

"Look," Phil said, drinking his coffee. "I don't want to tell you this. I'm happy letting this all play out, but I legally have to."

"Tell me what?"

"Your life is in danger."

Peter laughed.

"I can't tell you the whole story, but there's been a hit or-dered on you. Is Nicky your enemy now?"

"I don't have any enemies."

"Look, your life is in jeopardy, asshole. Don't go home for a few weeks. Let this thing die down."

Peter thought this was a game the police were playing, so he ignored the warning. What Peter didn't know, and wouldn't until decades later, were the steps the Jade Squad was taking to protect Kid Jai's life.

The Jade Squad had an informant inside the White Tigers named Ernie Young. Ernie had been part of several meetings concerning the assassination of Kid Jai. The Jade Squad knew the car that was going to be used and they knew the shotgun that would be used. In a creative effort on the part of the Jade Squad, the city had the car in question towed and brought to an impound lot. When this happened, the ATF replaced the shotgun shells in the gun with blanks. They allowed the car to be recovered with the shotgun full of blanks.

Kid Jai's normal safety precautions were enough that the plot to assassinate him never unfolded. If it had, his enemies would have shot Kid Jai with a shotgun loaded with blanks.

Shortly after this, Mongo sat down Taiwan and Peter Chin and had them discuss their differences. With Mongo there to show that neither one had any reason to distrust the other, they made peace.

Peter became the go-to guy in the New York Asian entertain-ment business. He had many business ventures and projects, but the phone call from Chow Yun-fat had nothing to do with business.

Chow Yun-fat was already a popular action star with his fame on an upward trajectory. At two o'clock one morning in 1983, Peter's phone rang, waking up him and his wife.

"Hello?" Peter answered groggily.

"Kid Jai, this is Chow Yun-fat. I need to ask if you've seen my girlfriend."

Peter sat up, struggling to clear his mind as he tried to make sense of the question.

Peter was becoming accustomed to the Hong Kong entertainment world always needing something. His company, Oriental Arts, was getting involved in many projects, but as Peter listened, he realized that this wasn't a business call but a personal one.

"Is she in the United States?" Chow Yun-fat asked nervously.

Peter was pretty sure that the woman he was asking about was in the United States and was even more sure that she wasn't Chow's girlfriend any longer. She was involved with Peter Chan, a prominent entertainment promoter. The tabloids had been keeping tabs on her as paparazzi followed her around constantly.

Peter had an idea of who she was probably with and where, but he had to stay out of situations like this.

"This is a personal matter between you and her. I cannot help you."

Peter got off the phone.

The shooting at the Golden Star bar at 51 East Broadway created a domino effect that ran through Chinatown and altered—as well as ended—many lives. Because of Chinatown's mistrust of outsiders and the language barrier between it and the rest of New York and because of the media and police errors in dealing with Chinatown, the public had multiple versions of the event itself, as well as its aftermath. Even today, beliefs include various theories about the Ghost Shadows and the On Leong Tong's involvement.

Chinatown knew the basics of the truth, and Peter Chin was able to piece the rest together from his unique vantage point. It all began with Herbert Liu.

Herbert Liu was a former Hong Kong police officer who'd immigrated to New York's Chinatown. According to Peter, Herbert wasn't really a street guy but a successful businessman. He was the first to see the value of the newly formed Resorts Casino in Atlantic City and organized lucrative junkets from Chinatown to Atlantic City for gambling and entertainment, later on becoming involved in booking these events world-wide.

To give an idea of how successful this venture was: Peter had once stood behind Herbert Liu in line at the bank and over-heard Herbert depositing a million dollars in cash into one of his accounts as casually as someone cashing their weekly pay-check.

For some reason, Herbert Liu yearned to be part of the Chinatown underworld, and he became a member of the Hip Sing. Then there was a business deal that Herbert wanted to go in on with Uncle Benny. Uncle Benny said no. Herbert felt that Uncle Benny was being too old-fashioned, too stuck in his ways. Herbert Liu left the Hip Sing and created his own street gang, the Freemasons, recruiting former members of other gangs and individuals forced out of existing gangs, as well as civilians, with the promise of a cut of Chinatown's plunder.

The Freemasons became the Chinatown farm team, the minor league of Chinatown crime, where the hopefuls along with the has-beens could get in on a ground-floor opportunity of a new criminal organization.

Herbert Liu located his unsanctified gang in the outskirts of Chinatown proper: East Broadway and Chatham Square. Iron-ically, the same streets the Ghost Shadows had worked hard to move out of were the ones in which Herbert Liu saw great po-tential. The Freemasons grew, and with that, so did their close association with Stinky Bug's new White Tigers, and soon Uncle Benny could not allow this disrespect to go unanswered.

"A helicopter goes up fast," Uncle Benny said when refer-ring to Herbert Liu, "but it comes down just as fast."

Working back from the events that came later, Peter Chin concluded that Uncle Benny had put out a contract. This was not specifically to kill Herbert Liu—if he happened to be killed, that was fine—but to teach him a lesson. Uncle Benny worked by going to one man, the top one, to give the order. He gave it to his godson, Michael Chen, the Scientist, the Dai Lo of the Flying Dragons, to teach Herbert Liu a lesson.

Although Herbert Liu did frequent the Golden Star, his movements were easy to track, so they likely knew he wasn't going to be there. It's highly unlikely that the Scientist himself, who kept himself quite insulated, was one of the three masked men who stepped into the Golden Star on December 23, 1982. On that date, these three men began firing into the crowd.

The gunfire and screams rang out inside the Golden Star as the masked gunmen pumped a barrage of bullets into the restaurant, killing three and injuring eight. The three killed were thirteen-year-old Stephen Chan, Michael Tsun, and Irving Woo, the White Tiger who tried to assassinate Peter.

Shootings in Chinatown during this time period were not rare, but this particular one drew national attention, and with it, national heat.

Hours after the Golden Star shooting, Chinatown found itself under the federal and state microscopes, and it was soon crawling with various agencies interviewing everyone they could find to collect information. Although the police and the feds were trying to determine what had happened and why, the true underworld of Chinatown already knew who had given the order. Some were already making plans to avenge it.

On the day after the Golden Star shooting, on December 24, 1982, Peter received a phone call from David Wong, a.k.a. Stinky Bug.

"I need to borrow your street," Stinky Bug said.

"Borrow my street?" Peter asked. Stinky Bug explained that the White Tigers wanted to cross Mott to get to Pell Street. Peter understood: The White Tigers and the Freemasons wanted revenge. They wanted to get to Pell Street and kill as many Flying Dragons as they could. Peter granted Stinky Bug access to the street.

When the White Tigers got to Pell Street, they realized that their attack had not been a secret. Not a single Flying Dragon was on the street. The White Tigers marched to the Hip Sing office, which at the time was at 16 Pell Street, hoping to meet a few Hip Sing there.

The Hip Sing buildings, usually busy with activity, were also completely abandoned. The White Tigers checked each room and floor and there wasn't a single person there. They destroyed everything they saw—paintings, incense, idols, paperwork—then they left.

The pressure in Chinatown continued to build from all directions. Instead of meeting with Uncle Benny to settle it, the Scientist dug in even more and was heard saying, "Godfather or no godfather, I make the calls." A definite sign of disrespect. If Peter and others were hearing this from their vantage point, then Uncle Benny definitely was.

Uncle Benny, seeing the pressure created from the Scientist's efforts as well as the possibility that this could lead authorities from the Scientist back to him, had enough reason to take his godson out.

The Scientist—always a very careful Dai Lo—switched his personal bodyguard to someone outside of the Flying Dragons, a man named Kai Ming Yuen from Boston's Chinatown. The Scientist knew Uncle Benny wasn't pleased with him and no longer trusted his own Flying Dragons to protect him. This step didn't help. The Scientist's bodyguard was killed six hours before the Scientist was killed.

The body of Kai Ming Yuen, the Scientist's bodyguard, was found on the Shelter Rock Road exit of the Northern State Parkway in New Hyde Park, Long Island. He was shot three times in his right ear and once in his left ear. His body was discovered by two sanitation workers.

Later that day, on March 13, 1983, Michael Chen, the Scientist, was found dead, tied to a chair with five bullet holes to his eye, at the Hip Sing Credit Union. The body was found at 12:30 p.m., when the Hip Sing Credit Union opened for the day.

In order for this murder to have taken place, the Scientist must have trusted whomever he was meeting there to show up without a bodyguard at all, and there must have been at least two people to tie him up. The only two people who had the key to the Hip Sing Credit Union were Uncle Benny and the Scientist.

Uncle Benny needed the two assassins of the Scientist gone as well, so there were no ties back to him.

One of the shooters selected was a Flying Dragon with the Chinese street name of Liang Jai, which translates in English to Youngest, who was also most likely one of the hit men who killed Peter Wong. The other hit man was Fun Bill, a classmate of Peter's, who got away with this crime for over a decade, moved to Los Angeles, and got a job in a bank, where he remained relatively unnoticed until a cold case squad in Los Angeles tracked him down in 1993.

The final domino to fall from the Golden Star incident wasn't revealed for another year. Prosecutor Nancy Ryan, the Jade Squad, and her team from the district attorney's office had been busy building a case against the Scientist and the Flying Dragons. This promised not only to seriously disrupt organized crime in Chinatown but also to be the very first Racketeer Influenced and Corrupt Organizations Act (RICO) case ever brought against any Asian organized crime group. With the Scientist gone, Nancy and her team moved the focus from the Scientist and the Flying Dragons to Kid Jai and the Ghost Shadows. Peter Chin was now the prime target for the Manhattan District Attorney's Office, which led to the biggest FBI raid on Chinatown organized crime ever.

* * *

Although Peter's entertainment business was booming, he kept his fingers on the street, forming a new crew of the Ghost Shadows based around a kid Peter was nurturing named Johnny Haung. Johnny knew nothing of the streets, but with Peter's help, the crew was growing and becoming successful.

With the Scientist gone, Peter wanted to know who was in charge of the Flying Dragons, so he made some inquiries. A few nights later, a Flying Dragon named Raymond Luk, a.k.a. Big Lip, walked into Peter's club, the Golden Taipei. He was introduced to Peter.

"Kid Jai," Big Lip said. "Someone would like to meet you."

"Okay," Peter said, knowing that Big Lip was with the Flying Dragons. "Have him come in."

"My boss says it's too noisy here; he'd like to go somewhere else with you."

Peter told Big Lip he'd come, and then five minutes later walked out the door. In front of the club, in the driver's seat of a Mercedes, was Fox, Michael Yu, a high-ranking member of the Flying Dragons. Fox looked behind Peter, expecting to see his guys with him, but Peter was alone. Instead of getting in his own car and following them, Peter got in the passenger seat of Fox's car. Fox, a little confused, shook Peter's hand and they drove away.

"I've heard a lot about you, Kid," Fox said, as they headed uptown. "You just got in this car without any worry. You've got a lot of balls."

"My guys know I'm with you. I'm not worried."

As they drove and talked, Peter asked the question he wanted to know. "So who is in charge of the Flying Dragons?"

Fox smiled. "I am."

"Good to know."

They drove to a French restaurant—Peter was beginning to like French food—and they had dinner and talked. By the end of that dinner, the war between the Flying Dragons and the

Ghost Shadows was over. It was the first peace between the two groups in twenty years.

Although peace existed between the Flying Dragons, White Tigers, and the Ghost Shadows, the streets of Chinatown were now filled with their new mutual enemy: federal and state agents.

It's unclear whether the agents and officers that had Peter and the Ghost Shadows under surveillance weren't very good at it, or that they simply wanted Peter to know he was being watched. It's possible they wanted to be seen—it seemed to Peter that they weren't trying very hard to be stealthy.

A garbage truck sat for hours outside of the Golden Taipei, emptying a single garbage can, over and over, into the back of the truck. When Peter used a pay phone to return a call from his beeper, one or two people suddenly appeared at the phones around him making calls, but they never bothered to actually put the quarters in. They started with fake calls in the middle of a conversation.

A certain car with a certain license plate had a fat guy and a woman in it in Queens. The same car was spotted in Brooklyn with two thin guys, and then later on, with a single man wearing glasses in Manhattan.

When Peter drove, two cars followed: one right behind and another one a few cars back. If Peter ran a red light, the car ran it, too.

The Jade Squad and the US attorney for the Southern District of New York were building their case against the Ghost Shadows. Peter knew this. But he didn't know how close they were until he was summoned by Uncle Benny. Peter went to 15 Pell Street, and Uncle Benny came outside to meet him. Uncle Benny's bodyguard stood back and allowed Peter and Uncle Benny to take a short walk privately down Pell Street.

"There's an indictment coming down for you," Uncle Benny said.

"When?" Peter asked

"A few months. It's big. I'd get prepared."

Peter did. The Ghost Shadows' house attorney recommended an office that handled large organized crime cases.

"Thirteen years," the lawyer guessed. "If everything goes to shit, you could be looking at thirteen years."

Peter smiled. He could do thirteen years, no problem.

The lawyer had no idea what this indictment would include and how different it would be from any he had ever seen.

CHAPTER 6
The Dinosaur Gets
Thirty-Five Years

When they come to arrest you, they always do it in the morning. From the local to federal levels, when officers and agents act on a warrant, the arrest happens early in the day. In the morning, there is a higher chance the suspect is at home, maybe still asleep, groggy, and docile. All desirable elements for a successful arrest.

Peter saw and felt the noose tighten, so he sent his wife and son to stay at Ida's mother's where they would be safe. Then he moved into a sixth-floor apartment in Brooklyn. He wasn't hiding from the feds, but why make it easy on them.

In the early morning hours of Sunday, February 17, 1985, the largest Asian racketeering mass arrest in US history took place. Twenty-five members of the Ghost Shadows were indicted on federal racketeering charges, all related to RICO, led by Attorney General Rudolph Giuliani and Assistant District Attorney Nancy Ryan and supported by the Jade Squad.

Three of the Ghost Shadows listed in the indictment were already imprisoned on other charges, and there were an additional seven whom authorities were trying to locate. This meant that twelve individual high-level arrests had to be coordinated for the same time on the same day.

With the most common time for arrests like these being

around seven in the morning, the FBI bumped Peter Chin's arrest up a little earlier, just to be safe. At five o'clock that Sunday morning, thirty FBI agents in full riot gear arrived at Peter Chin's Brooklyn apartment.

The idea of catching Peter Chin at home and docile at five in the morning worked, but not for the reason the FBI thought it would. Peter wasn't beginning his day at five, he was ending it. Peter was just thinking about heading to bed when there was a pounding on the front door of his apartment.

"FBI, open the door!" *Pound-pound-pound.* "We have a warrant." Before Peter could get to the door, the FBI used a battering ram to break it down. Thirty FBI agents, all wearing the standard FBI windbreakers, stormed in and handcuffed Peter Chin.

They secured the apartment and read Peter his Miranda rights. "What's the charge?" Peter asked

"RICO," they answered.

"Rico?" he asked, as they walked him out of the house to the awaiting squad car. "I don't know any Rico." Peter was driven to the FBI headquarters at 26 Federal Plaza and taken to the seventeenth floor. He was locked in a room until two FBI agents came to question him.

"You're looking at six hundred years, Kid, unless you cooperate."

Peter let this sink in a bit. He had never heard of such a thing. *Twenty to life,* sure, now that was a stiff sentence, but *six hundred years?* If you lived to be a hundred, you would have to die and come back six times to serve your sentence. This was the beginning of his understanding of how big a RICO case was.

Across the country, similar interrogations like this were occurring with the other Ghost Shadows who were in the RICO indictment. Not all of these arrests were successful, as several Ghost Shadows had been tipped off and escaped arrest. Six Ghost Shadows decided to avoid the indictment and become fugitives. One of them, hearing the agents arrive, ran to the roof of his house in his underwear and then jumped to another roof before the FBI could catch him. He was able to get down to the street, out of the city, and out of the country.

The arrest hit every major news agency from coast to coast, and Rudy Giuliani, Nancy Ryan, and the Jade Squad held several press conferences to discuss the case.

Ever since Peter Chin was thirteen years old, he had been preparing for either a long prison sentence or death. These were the only two paths for the life he had chosen. Peter had done his best to avoid the death part as well as arrest, but a long sentence was coming. While waiting for trial at the Metropolitan Correctional Center—MCC—in Manhattan, most inmates focused on defense. Not Peter Chin. Peter skipped the normal denial stage and went straight to acceptance and planning, even before he knew what sentence he was accepting.

The first part of this plan he wanted to discuss with his wife the next time she visited. This was a difficult discussion but a necessary one. The second part was more fun and began a focus that carried him through his time at MCC, his prison years, and the life that followed. Peter focused on one thing to pass the time in prison: food. Not just any food, but really good food.

Long-term prison time didn't frighten Peter Chin, but a life of sandwiches and salads—American food—*that* did.

The MCC facility is at 150 Park Row in Manhattan, close to Chinatown. In fact, on Peter's second day incarcerated there, he could hear the fireworks from Chinese New Year in Chinatown only a few blocks away. A few blocks away, where the best food in the world was made.

Peter made a deal with an MCC guard. If she went and picked up food orders for him each week, he would give her $200 for each trip. They called in the order, she walked two blocks to get it, and she bought the food and pocketed the difference. The arrangement worked well on both ends.

Getting the food into MCC had a few challenges. Peter wouldn't get food just for himself but for all his codefendants, but if the takeout containers were found, this would lead to a major investigation because items were brought in from the outside, and Peter would remain in segregation until the investigation was complete. Each bag, each container, had to be carefully folded into the trash cans and hidden to ensure they weren't discovered. Peter was careful and the food kept coming.

While picking up food from the guard, Peter saw a familiar face in the other wing. Nicky Louie, his old Dai Lo. It had been almost eight years since he had seen him. It didn't hit Peter until later that Nicky was there as part of his own RICO case.

In a fascinating chain of events, when a guard told Peter to sweep the entire floor where he was smoking. Peter did, but the guard wanted him to sweep even more. Peter threw a broom at him, which landed Peter in segregation for thirty days. There he was cellmates with Guy Fisher, the kingpin of the Harlem drug trade and Nicky Barnes's right-hand man.

Later on, who was his cellmate, but Nicky Louie. It's ironic that the prison system put two people who tried to kill each other as cellmates. Peter hadn't seen Nicky since he'd shot at him in the car chase.

"This must be a big case if you're here, Nicky," Peter said. No violence occurred, no bad feelings existed, and the two began to catch up.

One day, while the two were in the cell, Peter saw a scar on Nicky's face.

"Where did you get that scar?" Peter asked. "I don't remember it."

"You," Nicky said, showing the exit wound on the other side

of his face. "You gave it to me." He described when Potato had shot him in the gambling house behind the barbershop on Mott Street.

It wasn't until then that Peter knew that everything Potato told him about shooting Nicky was true. Peter had wanted to believe Potato, but it had all seemed so far-fetched.

One day when Nicky was at his MCC job delivering food trays, he noticed something that he relayed to Peter.

"There is a bar," he told Peter. "On one of the windows."

"There are bars on all of the windows."

"Yeah, but this one is off-center a bit. I think I can get my head through. If I can, I can probably get my body through." Nicky tested the theory a few days later when no one was around and reported back to Peter. They began to plan their escape from the Metropolitan Correctional Center.

With Peter's Chinese-food connection, it was easy to have a few things added to the orders undetected. Peter had a small saw and blowtorch hidden inside the food containers. The plan was for Nicky and Peter to get outside the window and then use a rope made of torn bedsheets to rappel the seven stories down to the street. They were close to executing their plan when Peter realized just how high seven stories was—*especially* high for someone afraid of heights to be hanging from a homemade bedsheet rope.

"If we were on the third floor," Peter said, "no problem. But this is too high for me. I'm out."

The MCC escape plan was scrapped. Now they had to secretly get rid of the saw and the blowtorch.

The core of any RICO case rests on making a connection between the individual in question and a criminal organization. Once you do that, once you show that this person has received funds, taken orders, or made decisions on behalf of this group, then you don't have to establish any actual individual criminal guilt. Connection alone is enough to get a RICO conviction.

Plus, you can ask for a stiffer sentence for the individual, based on the criminal enterprise itself.

The Mafia Commission Trial was going on at this same time, led by US Attorney Rudolph Giuliani, and took place in the Southern District Court of New York from 1985 to 1986. Its goal was to disrupt the Mob by incarcerating the key leaders of each family, which included Carmine Persico, Fat Tony Salerno, and Big Paul Castellano.

In 1985, Rudy Giuliani was just beginning to use this legal tool successfully, and because of that, very few criminal defense teams had any experience in defending a RICO case, or had a full understanding of how it really worked.

It also left for some interesting legal platforming.

Everything the Ghost Shadows were ever accused of doing, as well as everyone individually connected to the case, was added to the eighty-nine-page indictment that Peter was being personally charged with. This included when Stinky Bug, Sparerib, and Nicky Louie were planning to kill him. In the indictment, item 64(b) reads *The Attempt to Murder PETER CHIN, a/k/a "Kid Jai" by Shooting Him in Chinatown.*

Among other things, Peter Chin was being accused of the attempted murder *of himself.*

The biggest aspect of the RICO indictment, beyond extortion, robbery, and loan-sharking, were thirteen gang-related murders. This included the murder of Victoria Kwa at the Co-Luck restaurant when the Ghost Shadows shot at James Mui and the Flying Dragons.

Peter Chin spent eighteen months at MCC. In all that time, he never saw someone leave for court and not return. No one got bailed out, no one got released. MCC was not the end of the line, it was the beginning.

Back in Chinatown, with twenty-five of the highest-ranking members of the Ghost Shadows behind bars or on the run, Mott Street had an immediate gap. The crown jewel of Chinatown that was once guarded by dozens of Ghost Shadows to protect its valuable gambling assets was now wide open. Rival gangs saw this and moved in quickly but were unable to hold the street for long before it fell to another gang, who held it only for a short period of time themselves.

It took a Ghost Shadow soldier named Robin Chee to get organized and retake Mott Street. In a short period of time, the Ghost Shadows recovered Mott Street and were rebuilding what they once had. Robin Chee became the new Dai Lo of the Ghost Shadows.

MCC is a tall building. Every floor has a north and a south. Peter was housed on the north side. However, the number of inmates was at an all-time high, so when coming out of segregation, Peter was supposed to be taken back to Seven North, but they put him in Seven South. There, his new cellmate was another person who had once tried to kill him: Stinky Bug. Peter and he had long since reconciled. As soon as Stinky Bug saw Peter, Stinky Bug smiled.

"Guess what?" Stinky Bug asked.

"What?"

"The video store is still running."

Peter smiled, too. There was something about that little store still open and defying Vincent Jew and the Wah Ching that made them both happy. Vincent Jew, however, had branched out a bit. While Stinky Bug and Kid Jai were in MCC, on August 16, 1985, Dino De Laurentis released the feature film *Year of the Dragon*, starring Mickey Rourke. The film is a gritty detective story set in the underworld of New York's Chinatown. In the background, dressed as a slick but successful businessman, is Vincent Jew of the Wah Ching. His official involvement in the film is not known.

At MCC, life began to take on a routine. Every Wednesday, Peter's wife, Ida, came to visit. It was during one of these visits that Peter had that difficult conversation with her.

"I want you to file for a divorce," Peter said, handing her the paperwork he'd had the lawyers write up for him.

Ida sat there, stunned. "What?" she asked, not sure that she heard Peter correctly.

"However this turns out," Peter said, "I'm going away for a long time. I need you and Anthony to have a life, a good life." Ida reluctantly listened but did as Peter asked.

Another constant visitor to Peter at MCC was Johnny Haung, the young Ghost Shadow who Peter had recruited as part of his new crew.

"I want you to do two things for me," Peter told Johnny.

"Sure."

"I want you to dismantle the crew, and I want you to go legit."

Johnny Haung listened and obeyed his Dai Lo. The crew was dismantled, and Johnny built a business in the customs industry at Kennedy Airport.

Daily life at MCC followed a pattern, especially on court dates. On the day the inmate was due in court, guards arrived at their cell at four in the morning. The inmate ate breakfast and got ready. By five, they were in "the bullpen" to wait to be taken to court. They remained there until ten, when they were handcuffed and transported to court. Since Peter was going to the Southern District courthouse, they shackled all the inmates as a group and walked them through a tunnel that led from MCC to the court. John Gotti, who was in the bullpen at the same time as Peter, had his trial in Brooklyn, so they transported him by van, as they did with Carmine "the Snake" Persico.

After a day in court, you left and were taken back to the bullpen until seven in the evening, when they escorted you back to MCC. By this time, dinner had already been served, so they saved a tray for everyone in court that day. If you were due in court the next day, you repeated the process.

It made for a long physical and emotional day. Peter felt especially bad for Anthony "Fat Tony" Salerno, who was already seventy-four. Peter saw each time he and Fat Tony were in the bullpen together how much the day taxed the older man. Peter could also tell Fat Tony was getting tired when he smacked the guards with his cane.

Applehead surrendered to authorities, and Four Eyes was part of an elaborate plan that involved kidnapping Applehead in Taiwan and bringing him back to US soil. This left Mongo, Taiwan, Whiteface, Paul, and Lefty still fugitives.

Twenty-one of the twenty-five Ghost Shadows were to be tried together. Peter met frequently with his codefendants in an MMC conference room to develop a strategy.

"There are thirteen bodies in this case," Peter laid out. "A jury is not going to overlook that. Go to your attorneys and see what kind of a deal you can get if you plead guilty to a few charges. Here is the rule." Peter's face became stern. "You plead guilty, but no one cooperates, and no one rats on anyone else."

Everyone sat down with their own lawyers, and these attorneys went to Nancy Ryan. The deals were accepted. Nancy Ryan sent a message for Peter through his attorney, Susan Kellerman.

"She said that unless you plead guilty," Susan relayed, "all deals are off and she'll take it to trial."

When Peter was sure that all his codefendants were happy with the plea deals, Peter agreed to plead guilty to three counts.

The deals were accepted and the sentencing hearing for the Ghost Shadows was scheduled separately.

On October 25, 1985, at ten in the morning, the sentencing hearing for Peter Chin began in the US Southern District Court in New York. The courtroom was full. Nancy Ryan was there. Luckily, Peter's mother, Kiu Chin, was able to get a seat.

Peter was hopeful, knowing that Nicky Louie had received a fifteen-year sentence. *Fifteen years,* Peter thought. *That's great. I can do fifteen years.*

Soon it was time. Peter stood with his attorney, Susan Kellerman, as Judge Sweet addressed the courtroom.

"Nicky Louie may have been the dinosaur," declared Judge Sweet, "but that dinosaur laid an egg that became the monster that terrorized Chinatown. That monster is you, Peter Chin. Therefore, I sentence you to the federal department of corrections for a term of thirty-five years."

The gavel went down, and twenty-six-year-old Peter Chin heard his mother crying in the courtroom behind him.

It took three weeks for Peter to learn where he would begin his thirty-five-year prison sentence. He knew it would be a maximum-security prison and there were only five in the country at the time. The US Penitentiary in Marion, Illinois, which later became the country's first supermax prison, had a twenty-three-hour lockdown, so Peter was hoping he wouldn't go there. Nancy Ryan was pushing for Peter to go to the maximum US Penitentiary, Terre Haute, Indiana, one of the toughest prisons in the nation, as well as the farthest from New York. That ended up being the place. Peter was transferred from MCC to Terre Haute, but transferring in the prison system is not a direct path. Inmates are sent via prison buses that also have to stop and drop off inmates at other prisons. The trip from New York City to Terre Haute, Indiana, a distance of eight hundred miles that should have taken seventeen hours by car, took over a month by prison bus. Peter arrived at Terre Haute in November of 1987 and began serving his sentence.

The same time Peter began his transition to Terre Haute, Indiana, Godfather Nick began his weekly visits to Peter's family in Brooklyn. According to Peter's son, Anthony, Nick always came with gifts for the child, visiting and seeing what the family needed each week. Nick became such a part of the family that he was asked to attend a wedding of Peter's in-laws, where the first known photograph of him was taken. Nick continued these weekly visits, never missing one, until he stopped for cancer treatments.

Terre Haute, a maximum-security prison built in 1940, housed around 1,200 of the most violent offenders in the country. It also had handball courts, tennis courts, and even a miniature golf course. While Peter was there, an inmate was killed with a golf putter, so the miniature golf course was closed.

Since Peter didn't have a typical childhood filled with sports and games, the idea of sports in prison intrigued him. With absolutely no past training or experience, he soon became a competitive tennis and racquetball player.

At the time that Peter was in Terre Haute, the inmates self-segregated by race for protection. There were only three other Asians in Terre Haute at the time, one of whom was a Malaysian man named Mow, whom Peter befriended.

Mow worked in the kitchen, not in the mainline kitchen, but in Terre Haute's kosher kitchen. Whereas the mainline kitchen served over a thousand inmates, the kosher kitchen— a smaller work area with two refrigerators and a small burner and stove—was where the kosher meals were prepared for the dozen or so inmates that required it. The kosher meals were known to be larger and higher quality. In the mainline kitchen, inmates were served one chicken leg with a meal, but in the kosher kitchen, inmates received the entire hen. Most of the kosher inmates had Italian last names. Peter estimated that of the dozen inmates who received kosher meals, only two of them were actually Jewish, and only one of them actually went to the Sabbath prison services.

As Mow was preparing to be transferred to another prison, he suggested that Peter take his job in the kosher kitchen. Peter liked the idea, knowing this would give him an opportunity to smuggle food back to his cell, and it sounded like interesting work. Peter learned that the one thing you didn't need to cook in a prison kosher kitchen was any knowledge of kosher cooking or Judaism. Mow didn't seem to have any.

One day, a Hasidic rabbi was touring Terre Haute Prison and walked into the kosher kitchen unannounced. The rabbi looked over Peter's shoulder to see what food was being prepared and saw what Peter was cooking that day: bacon.

The rabbi's screams filled the room. Peter jerked around to see a man he had never seen before, in full Hasidic robes, with his hands above his head, screaming. The rabbi ran down the hallway to get the prison administrator.

Shit, Peter thought, not sure who that person was or why he was screaming.

A few minutes later, the food administrator and the rabbi returned to the kosher kitchen.

"Chin," the food administrator asked, "did you cook bacon on that cooktop?"

"Sure," Peter answered.

The rabbi groaned and began pacing nervously.

"You know that kosher meals don't include pork, right?" the administrator said.

"Um, no."

Peter had to go through the process of showing the administrator and the rabbi how he'd cooked the bacon.

"What cutting board did you use?" the administrator asked.

"That one," Peter pointed, and the cutting board was thrown in the trash.

"What spatula was used?"

"That one," Peter said, and that spatula was thrown in the trash.

When all the utensils were replaced, the rabbi and the food administrator left and Peter had to begin cooking for lunch again. Peter knew a great deal about cooking from working with his sisters, but that was Asian food. Peter knew very little about American cooking, but he did see in the mainline kitchen that they made something called hamburgers. That seemed easy enough.

In the mainline kitchen, they had prepressed burgers, but in the kosher kitchen, they had ground beef that could be turned into patties. Peter began making the burgers and cooking them. He remembered the second part of the burger, cheese, so he added cheese. This is when the rabbi came back.

Peter heard the scream again, turned, and saw the rabbi run back to the food administrator. Soon, the administrator and the rabbi were standing in front of Peter once again.

"Chin," the administrator said, trying to sound stern, but it was difficult because he genuinely liked Peter. "You know that dairy can't be mixed with meat, right? That's why we have the two refrigerators."

"Oh," Peter responded.

Corrections were made and Peter went back to work. The administrator decided to better monitor when the rabbi visited from then on.

In the federal penitentiary at Terre Haute, Indiana, Peter Chin met a man who changed his life. His name was Gene Melvin Jones, an inmate from Tallahassee, Florida, with a history of small misdemeanor crimes that built up over time. He was white, educated, focused, and determined.

Besides the three packs of Camel nonfiltered cigarettes that Gene smoked, washing them down with his twenty-six cups of black coffee—Peter actually counted one day—*words* were the most important thing in Gene's life. Gene was in love with the power of *words*, more than anyone Peter had ever met.

Peter Chin, who had spent one day in school in Hong Kong and had dropped out of American school when he was thirteen, had little use for the written word. Unable to read in either English or Cantonese and able to speak only a broken English he had picked up, written words were something that Peter knew existed, but he had people to handle them for him. As a result, Peter was unable to read and fully understand his own indictment. Gene Melvin Jones changed that.

Gene taught the GED classes at Terre Haute and he and Peter became friends, then cellmates. Gene looked through Peter's indictment and explained a lot of it to him but did not hide the fact that Peter needed to learn to read and speak English.

"You know what Shakespeare said about words, right?" Gene asked.

"Who's Shakespeare?"

Gene gaped at Peter, stunned. "We," he said calmly, "have a lot of work to do."

From lockdown at 10:00 p.m. to 3:00 a.m. every day, Peter and Gene studied. Without many books to use as reference, Gene taught Peter to read using Peter's indictment—the mammoth pile of paper provided a great teaching aid—along with his thick copy of *Black's Law Dictionary*.

"Where does it say that?" Peter asked as he flipped through the thick indictment.

"Right there." Gene pointed while lighting up another Camel. "See the words? Read them to me."

Peter did.

Peter worked hard with Gene and soon the words and letters came to life for him. Peter began to see the world from the page, and then the world all around him opened up. He began to speak these words, read these words, and even write these words. His conversations to inmates became longer and he asked questions. The words kept coming.

Peter Chin and Gene Jones became close. Peter realized that if Gene had a weakness—besides the Camels and black coffee—it was booze. One might think that booze would be difficult to get in a maximum federal prison, but it was everywhere. Applesauce, peaches, raisins could all be easily fermented and made into a powerful alcoholic concoction. When Gene had a few hits, it was enough to change the intelligent, mild-mannered, bookish man to someone completely different.

A few hits of jailhouse hooch and the 110-pound Gene filled with rage and walked up to a 300-pound inmate with six life sentences.

"Are you looking at me?" he screamed. "It looks like you're

trying to stare me down, asshole." Luckily, the inmates had a strong sense of respect for Gene because he was helping most of them get their GEDs and because of his age, but Peter always kept an eye out whenever the man had a few drinks.

Peter got to see the true power of Gene's words the day that the warden came to the floor. The warden never came to this part of the prison, always remaining in the offices beyond, but the one time that he did, he walked right up to Gene.

Shit, Peter thought. *This can't be good.*

"Gene?" the warden said. "Can I have a word with you?"

This was enough to get everyone's attention. Having the warden here was rare, but having the warden walk up to Gene and ask to have a word with him?

"Gene," the warden spoke in a low frustrated tone. "They've frozen my assets. My wife can't get money for groceries. I'm begging you, please drop this lawsuit."

While in prison, Gene had begun a lawsuit. That lawsuit had developed into such a high level that the warden was now under financial scrutiny.

"I can't even use my credit cards to get Christmas presents for my kids," he pleaded. "Gene, if you drop the lawsuit, I'll get you transferred to any prison you want, anywhere. Tell me where you'll be the most comfortable and it's done."

Gene listened.

Gene looked at the warden, thought about the case, and agreed. He dropped the lawsuit. Not for any perks, not for a transfer, he just dropped it.

"Words did that?" Peter asked later on when they were in their cell.

"Words are the most powerful thing there is." Gene lit up another Camel from the butt of the old one.

With the lawsuit gone, Gene returned to preparing students for the GED, teaching his personal student, Peter, and finding grammatical errors in books that he could contact publishers about.

Peter's job at the kosher kitchen was going well. Besides Mow leaving him the job, Mow also left Peter something more lucrative: his poker game. Mow had a regular poker game in prison that Peter, with his in-depth knowledge of creating illegal gambling houses in Chinatown, was able to expand and make more profitable.

In prison there are certain things that are not tolerated. The top of this list is drugs and weapons. If you are caught with either, it would land you in segregation and could add additional criminal charges to your sentence. Gambling was a gray area that, if not outright encouraged, was almost legitimized. The prisons knew that you weren't going to stop gambling in prison. As long as no one got hurt, it was allowed. In Terre Haute, Peter didn't simply run a daily poker table, he began a gambling business.

Peter opened up his poker table daily. If for some reason he didn't, inmates sought him out to find out why. Peter, as the house, got 10 percent of every bet, win or lose, just for covering. This meant that in 1987, while he was in USP Terre Haute, a maximum-security prison, he was making $700 a day.

Since prisoners don't walk around with cash, Peter issued credit, usually around $2,000, but depending on the inmate, up to $10,000. If the inmate won big, Peter had people on the outside who either deposited the winnings in the inmate's commissary account or got it to family members or friends. If the inmate lost big, Peter had ways on the outside for funds to be returned to him.

It's worth noting that no one refused to pay on a bet in prison. Peter never had to seek an inmate out for nonpayment, and he always paid winners quickly. People simply paid as agreed.

The next gambling expansion that grew beyond poker was unexpected. Growing up, Peter Chin had no exposure to American sports. He didn't play them, he didn't know the rules of them, he didn't really like them. In prison, Peter intensely studied the gambling aspects of these sports. He read every article, watched every TV broadcast, listened to every radio interview. He soon knew which coach didn't react to pressure and what college fullback was having legal issues. He became an expert on the games and one of the most profitable handicappers. All sports bets went through Peter, and he rarely did not have the spread set to his advantage.

Ten years later, while Peter was finishing his final stint in FCI Allenwood, he was curious about how much he'd actually made in gambling from prison.

"Go back a year," Peter told the inmate who ran his books for him. "Take out all the losses and see how much was made in profit for one year."

The inmate did. When he'd finished, Peter learned that that particular year, 1995, yielded Peter $160,000 in profit from his gambling operation. In prison.

Barry Slotnick was a powerful criminal attorney who had represented John Gotti, Bernhard Goetz, Joe Colombo, and Manuel Noriega. He was also the Hip Sing's house attorney. Uncle Benny hired Slotnick's team to begin the appeal process for Peter's RICO case. Meetings were set in Terre Haute with the legal team.

Based on the legal fees Peter was quoted from attorneys of Barry Slotnick's stature a few years earlier, the fee for this was around $250,000. Uncle Benny picked up the tab.

The attorney met with Peter, listened, and gave his expert legal advice.

"I think you should cooperate." The attorney adjusted his cuff links and leaned back in his chair. Peter stared at the man in wonder, amazed at what $250,000 worth of legal advice can get you. Peter ended the meeting.

Robin Chee began visiting Peter in Terre Haute. Robin told Peter about everything that was going on within the Ghost Shadows. Peter ran into other Ghost Shadows as they were arrested and began painting the picture of Chinatown's current landscape. After he was transferred to Petersburg, Virginia, he had an order for Robin.

"Make this your last visit," Peter demanded. "These indictments run about every ten years, and it's been ten since the last one. RICO is coming. With the drugs you guys are dealing with now, sentences will be stiff."

Robin held his stare, not denying the drug involvement. "You'll be looking at life," Peter emphasized. "I hear things. If I can hear from here, that means the feds are on you like a hawk."

Peter stood and paced. "The way I see it is, you have three choices, Robin. One is cooperate and be a rat, which I'm hoping you never do. The second is take it to trial and fight it all the way. Three is make as much money as you can and run."

Peter lit a cigarette. "You need to make your decision, but you also need to get prepared. RICO is coming down on you. You need to distance yourself from me."

Robin obeyed his Dai Lo and didn't return.

When the arrests came later on, Robin took option one.

For three years, Gene worked with Peter on learning and mastering the English language.

"You speak like a Boston lawyer now," Gene said.

"I speak like a kid from Chinatown who can now speak English," Peter corrected.

There had been a change in Peter over the last three years. The world was now something he could access, something he was a part of. Peter was excited about this but also sad that his teacher was leaving him. Gene Melvin Jones was being released from prison.

Peter knew little about Gene's personal life, but he did know that Gene had received only one piece of mail in his three years in prison, and that was from a prominent educational publisher, thanking Gene for a grammatical correction he'd found in one of their books. Gene was incredibly proud of this, and he carried the letter around for weeks. Gene had no family that he spoke of, received no visitors, and didn't receive any phone calls.

"Where will you go?" Peter asked.

"I guess I'll head back to Tallahassee," Gene answered.

Peter knew there was nothing for Gene in Tallahassee. Gene would go there because that's where he came from. Peter decided to change that.

Eager to pay his friend back for the kindness he had shown Peter and for the gift of being able to read, write, and speak in English, Peter began to make arrangements for Gene Melvin Jones.

When Peter called the Ghost Shadows' safe house on Mott Street, a voice he didn't recognize picked up the phone.

"Hello?"

"This is Kid Jai, who is this?"

There was a pause, then a whisper, and the phone was handed to someone else.

"Kid?" Robin Chee answered cheerily. "How are you?" Too cheerily.

"Robin, who answered the phone?"

"Um, I'm not sure, probably just one of the guys who—" Peter could tell that Robin was hiding something from him.

"Who was it?"

Robin paused. He wouldn't lie, but he knew that Peter wasn't going to like the answer.

"That was Kenny. Kenny Wong."

Kenny Wong. Peter Wong's son. The man he'd promised he would look after his family after the shark fin incident. Now Kenny was running with the Ghost Shadows?

"I'm not happy about this," Peter said.

"I know, and we tried to keep him away, Kid, he just—"

Peter interrupted and got to the point of the call.

"I need you to do something for me." Peter told Robin what he needed.

When Gene Melvin Jones was released from the penitentiary in Terre Haute, Indiana, he did not go to Tallahassee, Florida, but took the bus from Indiana to New York. When he arrived in Brooklyn, Robin Chee was there to pick him up.

"Any friend of Kid Jai can't be walking around in rags." Robin handed Gene a $2,000 handmade leather jacket. Gene tried it on, feeling the fat envelope in the pocket of the jacket.

"There's some walking-around money in there, too." Robin grinned.

Robin took Gene to a condo owned by the Ghost Shadows. "You can stay here as long as you want." Then Robin had a lapse in judgment. He assumed that Gene was a street guy, a career criminal, and he handed Gene a .38 revolver. "Here's something else for you to feel safe."

Gene managed not to look shocked at the gun and tucked it in the pocket of his new leather jacket. When Robin left Gene, two events occurred that could have changed things if they'd occurred in a different order. If Gene had decided to buy the bottle of bourbon *after* he got cigarettes, then he would have already been mugged and wouldn't have had the funds to do so. But he didn't. Gene bought the bottle first, brought it back to the condo, then went back out to get cigarettes.

Gene Melvin Jones, from Tallahassee, Florida, didn't think it strange to pull out an envelope fat with cash in full view of everyone at the convenience store in Brooklyn, New York, while buying cigarettes. One of the store patrons noticed the money. He followed Gene out, threatened him, and took the envelope.

Gene, embarrassed and angry, went back to the condo where the bourbon and the gun were waiting for him. He proceeded to get very drunk. Then he shot up the condo.

A few days later, Robin Chee went to check on Gene. He found the bullet holes in the ceiling of the condo and an empty bottle of bourbon, but no Gene. Robin never heard from Gene again, and Gene never reached back out to Peter Chin.

For decades, there were three forms of currency that inmates used within the US prison system. The first was cigarettes, a highly valued and stable payment for commerce. The second was postage stamps, which were easily tradable and also held their value. The third currency was quarters and dimes. Each week, an inmate could use their commissary account to purchase one roll of quarters and one roll of dimes, a total of $15, up to $60 a month, to be used in the vending machines and pay phones. This was the official use for these quarters and dimes, but the unofficial use was for gambling or for purchasing black market items, drugs, homemade alcohol, and weapons.

In 1988, the prison system determined that the use of these coins caused too many additional concerns—beatings and even deaths. They banned the sale of rolled coins in all prison commissaries.

Soon loose change was rare, then it was considered contraband, but it decreased in prison value. In 1988, Peter Chin had a somewhat useless treasure trove of quarters stockpiled from gambling profits, including two full five-gallon industrial buckets, a total of $2,000 worth of quarters, that a prison guard was hiding for him. Once the ban went into place, the street value of these quarters increased. Having them discovered was a bigger risk. Now there were only two remaining forms of currency inside prisons: cigarettes and stamps.

Prison officials don't like to let inmates reside in one prison for too long. On April 19, 1989, Peter learned that he would soon be transferred to a different prison. That same day, more than thirty East Harlem teenagers were roaming New York's Central Park assaulting bicyclists and damaging park property. A few hours later, the raped and bleeding Trisha Meili, a twenty-eight-year-old Wall Street investment banker, was found naked and bound. She had lost 80 percent of her blood, had multiple skull fractures, and was rushed to Metropolitan Hospital, where she remained in a coma for twelve days.

When Trisha Meili came out of the coma, she had no memory of the incident, but by then the city was enraged by the narrative of wild African American and Latino youths preying on the innocent, hardworking people of New York. Trisha Meili became the symbol of the lawlessness in New York as well as of the country at large.

New York's Thirteenth Precinct immediately focused on the large group of youths who were in the park, and from there, on five specific ones, aged fifteen and sixteen. These five were questioned for over seven hours, without legal counsel and in some cases without their parents present, until the five youths repeated back an agreed-upon version of a confession.

Within hours of the confession, the five retracted their statements, stating that they had been intimidated, coerced, and lied to. Although the confessions were videotaped, the hours of interrogation that led to them were not.

On August 21, 1989, two days after the rape and assault in Central Park, the *Daily News* published a front-page article that read "WOLF PACK'S PREY: Female Jogger Near Death after Savage Attack by Roving Gang."

Nancy Ryan took this case with the same drive that she had with the Ghost Shadows and Peter Chin's RICO case four years earlier, determined to see justice done and pursuing the stiffest penalties possible for these five. She had her work cut out for her, because besides the confessions, there was no physical evidence of the five being involved in the crime in any way: no DNA evidence, no witnesses, no past histories of violence.

Nancy Ryan and the Manhattan District Attorney's Office rolled up their sleeves and went to work.

After four years in Terre Haute, Indiana, Peter was transferred to the Federal Correctional Institution in Petersburg, Virginia. This was closer for Peter's mother to be able to visit him.

It was an emotional day when Kiu Chin got to see her son. By then cancer had taken hold of her and she was not in the best of health, but Peter loved being able to spend time with his mother.

"Promise me something," Kiu asked her son.

"Anything."

"When you get out, even if I'm not around—"

"Don't say that."

"Even if I'm not around, promise me that you'll move back to the apartment on East Broadway. It's your home."

Peter wanted to ask, *What about the Cow, the man that still lives there?*—but he didn't. Since his release date was still a long way away, Peter agreed.

Life in Petersburg formed a routine. Soon, Peter established his poker table and found people to play racquetball and handball with. One of these handball partners was Sonny Franzese, the underboss of the Colombo crime family. Sonny was in great shape for a man of seventy-two and was a very competitive handball player. Of course, Peter was a third his age and twice as fast, but out of respect for the older man, Peter tamed his competitive drive to win.

Sonny had been released from prison years earlier, but while in New York at a diner, Sonny had seen a man he knew who stood up to greet him. Sonny shook his hand and walked to his booth. That man was under FBI surveillance and the photo of him shaking his hand was enough to violate Sonny's parole, since he had associated with a felon.

Ironically, inside prison, Sonny didn't associate with members of the other Five Families. He was civil, he'd say hello, but after his job serving lunch in the officers' mess hall, he'd go out in the yard to play handball or talk to Peter or Joe Whiskey. Joe Whiskey's real name was Joe Malino, and although Joe was Italian, he wasn't a Mob guy. Sonny seemed to prefer the company of people who weren't Mob-connected.

One day, Peter and Joe Whiskey were watching Sonny play handball in the yard at Petersburg.

"Do you see that?" Peter asked.

"See what?"

"Every time Sonny goes to serve, he rubs the ball twice on the wall."

Joe Whiskey watched, and the next time Sonny was about to serve, he rubbed the ball twice on the wall. "Holy shit."

Peter laughed. "I don't know if it's superstition or what, but he does it every time."

Joe Whiskey was a fixture at Petersburg. His day consisted of getting up, watching Sonny play handball, talking to Sonny and Peter, then going back to his cell. One thing that Joe Whiskey did love—one of his main vices—was bacon. Once Peter knew this, Peter cooked a bag of bacon up for Joe and brought it to him. After lockdown, Joe happily sat in his cell, eating his bacon.

Peter liked Joe. One time, when it was getting close to Christmas, Peter asked Joe a question.

"Joe, if you could have anything for Christmas, what would it be?" Peter expected Joe to say *more bacon*, but the answer surprised him.

"I would love," Joe said dreamily, "a shot of Crown Royal."

Peter decided to get this for Joe as a Christmas present. Getting items like this inside of Petersburg Federal wasn't as difficult as doing so at Terre Haute, because Petersburg was a medium-security prison, but it took a little finesse and the right connection with the right guard. One of Peter's most reliable guards was a big man named Larry. Larry was without a doubt the biggest human being Peter had ever met and was an intimidating prison guard. Peter had Larry pick up cash from the outside and smuggle it in for Peter, or had him make gambling payments to inmates' families. If Peter had Larry pick up $1,000, Peter let Larry keep $200 for himself. Peter knew the guards at Petersburg didn't make very much, and he liked Larry.

Peter reached out to Larry, and he agreed to get the Crown Royal. The next day, Peter watched as Larry came in. He was holding the pair of sneakers that he would change into when he left, but nothing else.

Shit, Peter thought. *He forgot the Crown Royal.*

Peter met up with Larry later.

"You couldn't get it?" Peter asked.

"I got it." Larry reached under his desk and lifted up his shoes. Inside one of the giant size-sixteen shoes was the Crown Royal. The round bottle fit perfectly inside the large man's shoe.

Two days later, Joe walked into his cell and saw an entire bottle of Crown Royal on his table.

Joe Whiskey couldn't believe it.

"The only thing I ask," Peter said, "is that when you're done, give me back the bottle. I'll have to be careful how I get rid of it." When Joe finished the bottle, Peter broke it up into smaller pieces and buried it in various locations throughout the yard.

A few months later, Peter got in trouble and was sent to segregation. Without Peter to provide for him, Joe went looking for his own source of bacon. The next day, Joe Whiskey was found dead in his cell along with an empty bag of cooked bacon. Peter always felt responsible for this, not knowing if maybe the bacon quantity had been higher than what Peter normally gave the man.

Back in New York, in two separate trials in 1990, with the evidence stacked against her but public opinion on her side, Nancy Ryan was able to get a conviction against the Central

Park Five. Since the five were all minors, they were sentenced to ten years each. The public was outraged at how light of a sentence this was.

Peter noticed over the next several months that Larry the prison guard was getting thinner.

"You don't look so good," Peter said.

"Cancer," Larry answered. "Not much they can do, but I still have to work."

A few days later, Peter had Larry pick up $2,000 from outside the prison.

"Where does it go?" Larry asked.

"To you," Peter told him. "I want you to have it, for medicine or bills or whatever you need."

The two men looked at each other for a few moments until Peter broke the silence. "I'm sorry you're sick."

Larry was silent and walked away. Days later, he found Peter.

"You know Pete," the big man smiled. "All my coworkers know about the cancer, it's no secret, and I don't expect nothing, but you're the only one who did anything for me."

Larry worked for another three months until the cancer forced him to seek long-term care. He died shortly after.

On August 27, 1990, twenty-nine people were indicted by a federal grand jury on charges of operating a nationwide illegal gambling operation. Eddie Chan was listed, but he had been a fugitive for six years and his whereabouts were still unknown. Charges included racketeering, conspiracy, illegally conducting a gambling business, filing false tax returns, bribery, collection of unlawful debts, and the solicitation to commit murder.

The indictment was the result of a two-and-a-half-year investigation by the Internal Revenue Service and the Federal Bureau of Investigation. It included defendants in New York,

Chicago, Houston, Detroit, Minneapolis, Pittsburgh, and Atlanta.

Four chapters of the On Leong Merchants Association, including the national chapter, were involved.

In discussing the absent Eddie Chan, one law enforcement official referred to Eddie as "the John Gotti of Chinatown."

Two former presidents of the National On Leong Chinese Merchants Association, Yu Lip Moy and Chan Wing Yeung, were released on a $1 million bond after appearing in the federal district court in Manhattan regarding the indictment.

CHAPTER 7
Back to the Beginning

When he arrived at US Penitentiary, Allenwood, in Pennsylvania, Peter's first priority after getting his shower shoes, toothpaste, and everything he else he needed from the commissary was to identify the prisoner who was the kitchen's butcher. A partnership was arranged: Peter sent money to the butcher's family, and they supplied Peter with the meat he needed. Once he had his meat supplier, Peter got a job in the kitchen making salads, which gave him the chance to hide vegetables and access to the big walk-in cooler. In the cases of butter within that cooler, Peter kept his safety deposit box.

Pulling small boxes of butter out of the larger box created an insulated place to hide chicken, pork, everything he would use. The food was available and plentiful, but Peter soon hit a snag: a guard named Dennison.

"Go ahead and look," Peter said. Dennison, who was searching Peter's room, turned with two eggs in his hands.

"What are these?" Dennison asked.

"You're never going to find drugs or weapons in here," Peter said. "But you will find food. I've got to eat."

Most guards ignored it, not caring if Peter had a few potatoes or some carrots in his room. Dennison *did* care. Every violation was reported, every piece of contraband taken.

"What's this?" Dennison asked, walking from Peter's cell with an onion in his hand.

"Dennison, why you have to be this way? It's just food."

"Contraband." Dennison confiscated the onion.

There wasn't a food that Peter couldn't get into prison. Once, when he was washing thirty beautiful codfish to store them in a plastic medical pan, Dennison made his rounds.

"Chin!" he yelled. "What do you have there?"

Peter reacted quickly and ran out of the room with the pan of codfish. Peter, who was in great shape and played racquet-ball several hours a day, was much faster than the potbellied Dennison. Peter shoved the pan along the floor like a shuffle-board to a guy in his cell who quickly hid it under his bed.

Peter slowed down and let Dennison catch up.

"Chin!" Dennison screamed, his face red and voice labored. "Where is it?"

"Where is what?"

"Whatever you had."

"I didn't have anything."

"Then why did you run?"

"Because you were chasing me, Dennison. I didn't know why you were mad at me, so I ran."

Dennison wanted to report the incident, but he couldn't do so without physically having the contraband.

When Peter had enough of the raw materials from the kitchen, he made hundreds of dumplings for himself and the other inmates. Cooking in prison takes some creative tools, one of which is called a stinger. A stinger is a modified extension cord in which the positive and negative ends are separated. Once plugged in and dropped into a container of water, the stinger will soon have the water boiling.

Peter had the stinger ready to drop into a plastic bucket of water when Dennison walked in. With some quick thinking, Peter changed his approach.

"Dennison, great, I was just going to try to find you. You've got to try these dumplings. These are the best dumplings you'll ever have." Peter fixed Dennison with a stern look. "You've had Chinese dumplings before, right?"

"Yeah, I mean, I think."

"Forget about those, they are nothing like these. You've got to try them. I need your help."

Peter handed the stinger to Dennison. "Okay, hold that end in the water but don't let it touch the edge or it will blow up."

"Blow up?"

"Yeah, but you won't let it, you'll keep an eye on it."

Dennison sat there, holding the stinger as Peter cooked the dumplings. When they were done, Dennison tried one.

"Pretty good, huh?" Peter asked.

"Really good," Dennison answered.

Peter Chin was not reported that day, and a few days later, when Peter saw Dennison again, the guard called him over. "When are you going to make those dumplings again?"

Although still a rule follower, something changed in Dennison. One time, when he called Peter into the office, there was a pile of chestnuts on the desk. As they talked, Dennison turned so the chestnuts were exposed for Peter to take. Dennison couldn't break the rules by offering Peter the chestnuts, but he could allow them to be taken.

It was a start.

On July 23, 1994, while Peter was at FCI Allenwood, eighty-seven-year-old Kai Sui Ong, also known as Uncle Benny, was admitted to New York Downtown Hospital under a false name. Uncle Benny had been battling prostate cancer but now had pneumonia, which concerned his family and doctors. Under a pseudonym, Uncle Benny was kept in a private room with the hospital staff doing their best to care for him as well as protect his anonymity. These precautions didn't prevent word from reaching journalists that the Godfather of Chinatown might be nearing the end of his life. Maureen Flatley, hospital spokesperson, repeated the same line to the myriad of phone calls the hospital received from reporters: "There is no one by the name of Ong registered in this hospital."

This was true, but Uncle Benny was there. For almost two weeks, Uncle Benny's family sat with him as he remained hidden, weakening. On Saturday, August 6, Uncle Benny died.

Richard Eng, the executive secretary of the Hip Sing Association, confirmed Uncle Benny's death and announced that Chinatown would have a three-day funeral ceremony to honor the great man. On August 17, 1994, the ceremony began for the biggest funeral New York's Chinatown had ever seen.

After the service at Wah Wing Sang Funeral Home, Uncle Benny's bronze casket was carried to a hearse. Family, business partners, and dignitaries, including government officials from Taiwan, loaded into the 120 limousines followed by 5 Cadillac flower-cars to drive to the cemetery. The slow drive through Chinatown's narrow roads left traffic backed up for hours, and the streets were filled with mourners from Chinatown, Little Italy, and beyond.

Countless undercover police, some dressed like tourists, others in baseball caps and T-shirts, mixed in with the crowd.

The funeral procession stopped at 15 Pell Street, the Hip Sing Association, where the door of the hearse opened to allow Uncle Benny's spirit to leave.

Feature articles on the funeral appeared in all major newspapers from the *Washington Post* to the *New York Times*, and the event had major media coverage in Hong Kong and Taiwan.

After Uncle Benny's death, the tongs still existed but were often referred to as "the tigers without teeth." With the absence of the tongs, the developing RICO cases, and the need for the gambling houses to be more discreet, the tongs and gangs began losing their grip on Chinatown.

The same year Uncle Benny died, so did Peter's father, Bark Ching Chin, the Cow. Peter mourned the death of Uncle Benny but felt nothing whatsoever for his father's passing.

The knowledge of Uncle Benny's death triggered a thought that Peter finally permitted himself to acknowledge. He allowed the thought to come forward, examined it from all angles, and saw what it really was. He said the words to himself for the first time: *I'm not going back.* He knew this was the right choice.

Peter Chin would not go back to the Ghost Shadows or to the only life he had ever known. He had carried the flag long enough, he hadn't become a rat, he had done what he said he would do, he had paid the debts he owed.

In most criminal groups, the lower levels kicked up to the higher levels and fed the top. In the Ghost Shadows, the boss was responsible to feed the family below him. This burden meant that Peter was responsible for the physical and the financial well-being of so many people. Even ten years later, Peter sat in his cell and drove himself crazy thinking about it all.

When Peter realized that he wasn't going back to this life, part of the burden that he had carried vanished. Excitement and hope grew in its place. After all, if Peter had accomplished so much in the organized crime world, maybe he could do as much in the legitimate world?

Even though Peter wasn't getting out of prison anytime soon, this vision of a new life when he *did* get out was comforting. There were other guys in prison who couldn't give up on the idea that freedom was just around the corner. Herbie Sperling was one of those *just-around-the-corner* guys.

Herbie Sperling—whose criminal pedigree began with working with Dutch Schultz—was one of the first inmates who was sentenced to life *without parole.* With Peter, thirty-five years was considered *life.* Life without parole meant that you weren't going *anywhere.* Nevertheless, Herbie held on to that dream of getting out.

Every time Peter saw Herbie, he greeted Peter warmly with "Hey, Pete, I got a new appeal, I'm getting out soon." Peter smiled and listened to the latest legal work that was being done on Herbie's behalf.

Herbie Sperling was a convicted drug dealer from Hell's Kitchen who was found guilty of killing Vincent C. Papa, the mastermind behind the theft of four hundred pounds of French Connection heroine.

Herbie was in on a CCE charge, a continuing criminal enterprise involving narcotics. They called it the kingpin charge. The kingpin charge came with a mandatory life sentence.

The little cigar-smoking man worked out of a barbershop. Worried that the barbershop was bugged, when he needed to talk business, Herbie walked outside and leaned against a mailbox to talk. The feds wired the mailbox. From then on, every deal Herbie made was recorded.

Herbie Sperling never got out of prison. He died there at the age of seventy-nine.

The truly important rules in prison are not the administrative ones but the ones held by the inmates, which kept order and control. One rule has to do with where you sat during meals. There is a hierarchy in prison, a pecking order, and knowing who sits where, with whom, and when is important. Sitting in another man's seat can get you killed, as it is a serious sign of disrespect.

Another rule has to do with the TV room. Many prisons have multiple TV rooms, one designated for sports, one maybe set on movies, but the channels, the programs that are watched, are determined by the senior person in the room. Changing the channel, even if the TV room is empty, can also get you killed.

In Allenwood, there were four TV rooms: One showed sports, one was for movies, one showed the Black Entertainment Television Network (BET), and one the Spanish channels. Those genres were set in those rooms, designated by the prison itself with signs posted to reduce fights. Changing the channels within that genre was done through the senior person in the room. The one with the most clout. Changing the channel to something outside of the set genre was never done.

Peter was sitting in the movie room alone when Mayweather

walked in. His face was panicked. "Brother Kid," he asked, walking over to Peter with his hands folded. "Brother Kid, can I please change the channel?"

Peter thought this was strange. Mayweather had barely seen what was on—why did he want to change the channel? It didn't matter. Allowing the channel to be changed showed weakness and Peter couldn't have that.

"No," Peter said.

"My son," Mayweather went on. "My son has his first fight on HBO right now. It's just getting ready to start. Please, I need to see it."

"Fight?" Peter said. "Boxing? I hate boxing. Go to the sports room."

Mayweather moved in closer. "I did, but they're watching something else. It's his very first aired fight. I have to see it. Please, Brother Kid."

Peter looked at the man, thinking he was either out of his mind or playing some sort of con. He was bored with this show anyway.

"If I walk back in here and they don't announce your last name," Peter stood up. "That means that you lied to me and I'll kick your ass."

"Thank you," Mayweather said, moving quickly to change the channel.

A few minutes later, Peter walked back into the TV room, and yes, there was boxing on. They didn't have to announce the name. The young fighter in the ring looked just like his father, just like Roger Mayweather, who stood in the Allenwood Penitentiary TV room watching his son fight.

Peter sat down and watched. Roger Mayweather's son, Floyd, knocked out Roberto Apodaca in the second round. Roger was on his feet screaming.

One of the commentators remarked at the end, "There have been very few who have been more talented that this kid. He will probably win two or three world championships."

Peter looked over. Mayweather, the father, was beaming.

* * *

There was a new inmate in the compound. When Peter saw him, he thought he'd seen a ghost. It was Robert Hsu, a.k.a. Potato.

Peter approached slowly, still not sure if who he was looking at was real. "Potato?"

The man looked to the right through his thick glasses, then left, searching for the voice until he saw who was walking toward him.

"Kid!" Potato screamed, rushing to hug his old Dai Lo as he began to cry. "Kid," he repeated.

They embraced. Peter grasped Potato's shoulders and took a long look at him.

"I can't—" Peter swallowed tightly. "I can't believe it's you."

The tears in Potato's eyes were magnified through the thick glasses. The two hugged again and walked together to catch up.

"What happened to you?" Peter asked.

"You don't know, man," Potato said, and reached out to touch Peter's shoulder occasionally as they walked. "They sent me to Marion."

Peter knew that Marion Correctional Institution was the toughest maximum-security prison there was, a twenty-three-hour lockdown facility. Peter also knew that Potato was serving two sentences: the attempted murder of Nicky Louie and the Ghost Shadows' RICO. Nancy Ryan had offered Potato a deal. If Potato testified directly against Peter Chin, Potato would be granted leniency. Potato refused.

Potato was sent to Marion and placed in solitary confinement, twenty-three-hour lockdown, for years.

"The eyes need exercise." Potato explained his glasses. "They need something to focus on beyond a ten-by-five cell. I read all the time, but I had nothing faraway to look at, like a tree or a mountain. My eyes got bad."

Peter listened and then hugged his old friend again. "I'm glad you're here. We'll need to get you set up with a few things."

In prison, the only thing that travels with you is your "jacket," or your file; your money doesn't arrive until a week or so later. Potato needed several things to be comfortable at Allenwood Federal: shower shoes, a toothbrush—the government-issued toothbrush worked once before falling apart—toothpaste, sneakers, shaving cream. Peter got these things for his old friend and made arrangements to meet the next day, so Peter could give everything to Potato.

The next day, Peter had everything Potato needed. He saw an inmate that had come in with Potato but couldn't find the man himself.

"Hey," he asked the inmate. "Where's Potato?"

"It's weird," the inmate answered. "They transferred him out last night. I never seen them transfer one out in the middle of the night before."

The prison officials must have realized that Potato and Peter Chin were together in the same prison, which was likely against what the prosecutor wanted. They had transferred Potato that night to another prison.

On July 13, 2000, Kiu Ho Chin, Peter's mother, passed away after a battle with cancer. His sisters sent word to the prison chaplain, who in turn told Peter, so Peter heard the news the very same day.

In some cases, special arrangements are made for inmates to attend the funerals of close family members. Approval is granted and a federal marshal escorts the inmate to the service, stays with them the entire time, and then returns. Peter knew that the chance of this happening for him was rare, but he had to try. He went to his case manager and put in the request.

"Sorry, Chin," he said. "It's not even worth putting in the request. You're too high-profile."

Peter walked back to his cell and mourned the death of his mother from Allenwood Federal Penitentiary.

Life went on. One day Peter saw a new inmate who looked familiar to him. Peter approached him and the young man looked away, trying to find a way to escape, but it was too late.

"You look familiar," Peter said. The young man hung his head. Slowly, he looked up at Peter.

"Hello, Uncle," the man said. Peter realized who it was.

"You look like your father," he said. Peter looked at young Kenny Wong, son of Peter Wong of the shark fin incident.

"Why are you here?" Peter asked.

Kenny knew he couldn't avoid it any longer. "I'm a Ghost Shadow."

In 2002, Matias Reyes, who was serving thirty-three years for murder and rape, confessed to being the man who raped and beat Trisha Meili in Central Park in 1989. His DNA matched the DNA found on the victim. On December 19, 2002, the New York Supreme Court vacated the prior convictions, exonerating all of the Central Park Five.

The Central Park Five filed a lawsuit against the city for malicious prosecution, racial discrimination, and personal pain and suffering. The city settled for $41 million.

Nancy Ryan had left the Manhattan District Attorney's Office by this time and has not spoken publicly about the exoneration of the Central Park Five.

Being released from a long prison sentence is not always a question of legal appeals and successful court reversals. Many times it's a matter of math.

At the time Peter Chin received his thirty-five-year sentence in 1985, the *good behavior* clock began to tick.

Good time, or good behavior, is less *good behavior* and more *not bad behavior*. Every day you are *not* put into segregation, you are *not* in a fight, you are *not* written up, those days are taken off the back end.

During Peter Chin's imprisonment, he was up for parole six

times. He didn't bother going to the parole hearings in the beginning, but those around him encouraged it.

"What's it going to hurt, Pete?" his fellow inmates said. "You've got nothing to lose."

Fourteen years into his sentence, Peter went to his first parole hearing and was quickly turned down. The good behavior clock kept ticking along.

When quarters were banned in US prisons in 2008, this left two standard forms of inmate currency: stamps and cigarettes. In 2003, the Federal Bureau of Prisons announced that in the following year, smoking would be banned in all US prisons. Panic flooded the prison system. Inmates were less concerned about smoking being a violation (after all, what *wasn't* a violation) than they were about being able to get their cigarettes. This created an opportunity for Peter Chin. If Peter could build a large stockpile of cigarettes before the ban went into effect and could store them safely someplace inside Allenwood, then he could provide a high-demand product with a high profit margin. This plan had two challenges. The first was getting the cigarettes. The second was finding a secure place to store them.

Getting the actual cigarettes turned out to be the easier step. Importing a large number of cigarettes from the outside through his connections of prison guards was too costly and too risky. The answer was to get them from within. Peter found four inmates who didn't smoke.

"Want to make some quick money?" Peter asked his nonsmoking friends. The inmates agreed to his plan.

What's interesting is that when the prisons banned the use of quarters and loose change, the risk of owning that commodity caused the value to go down. However, when cigarettes were being banned the value went up, exponentially up.

A single brand-name cigarette would now be opened up and

the tobacco rolled out using toilet paper for rolling papers, with each new homemade cigarette going for twenty dollars. In 2005, one pack of cigarettes had a street value of three hundred dollars. Cigarettes became much more profitable than drugs.

When the ban was announced, the prison commissary allowed an inmate to purchase up to twenty packs of cigarettes, two cartons, a week. Each inmate began buying twenty packs a week and bringing them back to Peter. Soon, Peter was sitting on three hundred packs of cigarettes, which led him to the challenge of storing them.

Peter split them up. He gave one hundred fifty packs to a friend who worked in maintenance and had him hide the stockpile. He kept the rest someplace close. The ban occurred, and Peter began selling the cigarettes. Soon, he needed to refresh his stock.

"I'll need twenty packs of cigarettes," Peter told the maintenance man.

"Okay," the inmate responded. "I'll try."

Peter was confused. "Try? What do you mean, try?"

"Well, I hid them in the head of one of those big stadium-sized lampposts in the yard—the ones that need to be taken down with a cable and a locked crank. I can't get to them until a light bulb burns out and they get the request to bring the pole down and unlock that crank."

Peter went out to the yard and found some inmates playing softball. He picked the player with the strongest arm and paid him to break one of the bulbs with a rock. The pole had to be cranked down for the lamp to be replaced. Peter had his cigarettes.

At the time Peter was incarcerated, the law stated that an inmate had to serve "one-third of their sentence as a minimum, and two-thirds as a maximum." Once that occurred, you are "maxed out." Being maxed out means you don't need the approval of a parole board, a court filing, or a successful appeal. You simply cannot serve any more time.

After serving twenty years and six months in prison, Peter Chin maxed out. He was being released.

In April, Peter got his release date: June of 2005. He began preparing. Clothes were sent in from the outside, transportation arrangements were made, and paperwork was filled out.

The normal excitement that you would expect from a man who was about to breathe free air again for the first time in twenty-one years didn't happen with Peter. The reason was simple: Peter didn't believe he was getting out. He thought they would go through the actual release, but it was a very common psychological practice the government used: The release date was set, clothes were sent in, papers were signed, and the doors were opened. The inmate stepped outside the prison for possibly the first time in decades, then was handcuffed again to be arrested on a totally different charge. Peter had seen this happen many times to people he knew, and he fully expected that this was the plan for him.

On the day of Peter's release, he put his street clothes on, gathered his few possessions from prison, including his copy of *Black's Law Dictionary*, and went to be processed and wait in the bullpen. He was escorted to the gate, the prison door was opened, and Peter stepped out. He took one step and looked to the right. Nothing. He took another step and looked to the left. Still nothing. He controlled the urge to run to his son's car, waiting for him. Peter got in and Anthony drove away. The car was half a mile down the road when it hit Peter that he was actually getting out of prison.

"Holy shit," Peter said.

Anthony smiled and handed his father a pile of cash from the money. "You'll need some walking-around money."

A few miles down the road, Peter had Anthony stop at a gas station so he could use the bathroom. The concept of being out of prison was beginning to settle in and he had money in his pocket and an incredible desire to actually buy something. It had been twenty years since he'd bought something from a store. He didn't know what to buy, so he gave the gas station attendant $10.

"Thanks for letting me use your bathroom," Peter said.

For the first three months after his release, Peter lived in a halfway house in the Bronx. This house had a very strict curfew, and because of the heavy Bronx traffic, Peter was always nervous about being late. Peter was released on a ten-year parole, and one of the terms of this parole was that he needed to be gainfully employed. He found a job through a former Flying Dragon who owned a restaurant supply business. The man was so honored to have Kid Jai working for him that he didn't want Peter to do any actual work, to just show up. Peter compromised and spent the day walking the owner's dog.

Peter was anxious to see how much New York had changed. On his day off, he took a cab all the way up to One Hundredth Street in Manhattan. He got out and began walking down toward Chinatown, looking at all that had changed. The walk took four hours.

Once released from the halfway house, Peter fulfilled the promise he'd made to his mother and moved back into the apartment at 92 East Broadway. It was strange being back. Peter tried to settle in, but all he could hear was the screams of his father. The ghosts of the past were too strong. After two months, Peter moved out. As the sole owner of this rare rent-controlled property, Peter was offered a substantial sum to sell it. Wanting no money that ever came from his father, Peter simply signed the apartment over, giving it away. It was divided into two separate apartments.

After the restaurant supply job finished, Peter needed to find something more permanent. He'd never had a traditional job in his life besides helping his mother in the garment factory as a child. Peter's sister reached out to her cousin-in-law, who owned a construction company. She had always talked about her brother and asked if they would meet with him. The cousin-in-law agreed.

Peter was cordial and friendly, making the cousin-in-law a unique offer. "You don't even need to pay me. I just want to learn and I need to be on your payroll for parole, but I don't need the money. I will work very hard."

Who could turn down an offer like that? Peter Chin began his first traditional job at the age of forty-six, as a driver and general construction assistant. One of his first assignments was to get a few boxes of screws. Peter had never been to a Home Depot and could not believe how many types of screws there were: wood screws, metal screws, finishing screws, screws with different thicknesses. He'd never bought screws in his life. The self-checkout process was also complicated; he wasn't even sure how to pay without a cashier. The man behind him in line was so annoyed, he helped Peter check out.

Peter worked, learned, and took in this new world around him. Like everything Peter Chin got involved in, he jumped in deep and absorbed all he could. There was something new to learn every day. When there was a window to be hung, Peter wanted to be involved. When there were bricks to be laid, Peter wanted to see how it was done. In only a year, he had a strong understanding of the basics of construction, masonry, and carpentry.

The New York Chinatown that Peter returned to in 2005 was not the one he left in 1985. The borders had changed. Little Italy had gotten smaller—now it was only a small section of Mulberry Street—as Chinatown grew, expanding beyond Chinatown proper to a separate Chinatown in Flushing, Queens.

In the 1980s, New York Chinatown was dominated by Cantonese speakers, probably ten to one over Mandarin, Korean, and Fukienese. As immigration continued, there were more Korean, Fukienese, Taiwanese, and Vietnamese who settled in the new Chinatown in Flushing, and that area grew. Soon, Cantonese took a back seat to Mandarin in Queens, and then later in Manhattan.

The biggest change was the internal one, the behind-the-curtain structure of this new Chinatown. With Uncle Benny gone, the tongs lost their power. Without the tongs, there was no high-level police bribery to keep the illegal gambling houses open. Without the gambling houses, the gangs lost their main source of income and power. With RICO, leaders of these criminal organizations were serving long prison sentences.

The once powerful tongs and street gangs of New York's Chinatown were gone. What was more prevalent in 2005 than in 1984 was drugs. When he returned, Peter saw drugs everywhere. He had not yet met a waiter who didn't also sell drugs on the side.

What was strong in Chinatown was the memory of those days of the tongs and gangs. In 2005 Chinatown, Kid Jai was a legend.

Word got out that Peter Chin was released, and people wanted to meet him. Former members of the Flying Dragons, Hip Sing, Tong On, all wanted to sit down with Kid Jai. Some of this was business opportunities, offering Peter a chance to get in on the heroin business or other criminal enterprises, but mostly they wanted to meet and show their respect. A few known Triad members, Big Head and Rock-and-Roll, asked Kenny to set up an introduction between them and Kid Jai.

To return this respect, Peter accepted all the invitations. For four solid months after his release, Peter Chin did not eat dinner alone. Though he was flattered, Peter quickly realized what an exhausting process this was. People wanted to show respect, but they also wanted to be entertained, to hear the stories of the glory days.

Even Herbert Liu, the man who was the focus of the Golden Star shooting that led to the Scientist being killed, sought out and sat down with Kid Jai.

For ten years, from 2005 until 2015, Peter Chin was on federal parole. During the first few years of parole, he was under surveillance from federal and local authorities. As with RICO, it's unclear if these agents wanted to be seen or simply weren't focused on stealth. Peter thought it was funny that some of them actually wore trench coats.

Since selling the Golden Taipei nightclub shortly before the RICO indictment came down, Peter was asked to get involved in another club, one called Chopsticks, in Flushing, Queens. Chopsticks was a karaoke club, and Yoki, the goddaughter of Peter's girlfriend, wanted to buy it. She wanted Peter to be her partner because there were some issues with the bar. Peter checked it out and met with Steve, the owner. When Steve saw Peter, he smiled.

"I sat in your limo," he said, pumping Peter's hand. "When I was a kid on Mott Street. That white limo that sat there for months, the driver let us sit in it, and some of us got short rides."

They came to an agreement of $45,000 and shook hands, and Steve handed Peter the key to Chopsticks.

Danny Mo, Peter's old friend from Toronto, had risen in rank with the Kung Lok Triad. When Peter was released from prison, Danny wanted to come to New York to see Peter.

Danny could travel to Hong Kong twice a week without issue, but he was on the watch list with so many agencies that getting into the United States was much harder. Danny was stopped at the airport the first time, so he flew back to Toronto and tried to enter through Buffalo. This worked. He rented a car and drove to New York to see his old friend Kid Jai. They met at Chopsticks.

Peter tried to get Danny Mo a hotel in Manhattan, but everything was booked. He found a hotel in Flushing, a little less glamorous than the Manhattan ones, but it was clean and close to Peter's bar.

Peter helped Danny and his crew settle in their rooms, and

beers were passed around. Peter, not much of a drinker, had a sip of a Heineken with them to be sociable. Peter went down to the lobby, but when he tried to walk through the big glass doors to get outside, they were locked. Peter pushed at them, but they didn't move.

Peter walked to the front desk, which in that part of Queens was covered with bulletproof glass, and knocked on the glass.

"Hello?" Peter called. "Anyone there?"

Something stirred, then a very sleepy hotel clerk came into view from another room.

"I need to get out," Peter explained. The groggy attendant just stared at him.

"Your door is locked," Peter pointed. "I need to get out."

The attendant blinked, looked at the door, then back at Peter. He did this a second time before speaking. "But you just got here."

Peter stopped, trying to figure out if this old man was drunk or on something. "Yeah, I did, and now I'm leaving again. Can you buzz me out, please?"

The attendant continued to stand there, confused, looking at Peter and then at the locked glass doors. After a few minutes, all pretense of civility left Peter Chin.

"What's wrong with you?" Peter said. "Let me the fuck out." He started pushing on the locked glass doors, but they didn't budge. The attendant looked even more confused and repeated, "I don't understand, you just got here."

"I dropped my friends off," Peter explained slowly and loudly. "Now I'm leaving. You can't lock people in a hotel, you asshole, so open the goddammed door." The attendant still wasn't processing this request and stood there as if he was working on a complicated math problem. Peter got angrier, banging on the bulletproof glass. "Press the fucking button!" Nothing happened.

Peter banged louder and louder with no response from the attendant. He picked up a decorative Christmas tree and threw it at the bulletproof glass. "Press the button." He threw a potted plant, magazines, anything in the hotel lobby he could find. *"Press the button!"*

Finally, the attendant decided to do something. Instead of pushing the button to open the doors, the attendant called the police.

The conditions of parole are very simple. Any violation that required jail time, even a day, could take the ten years given to Peter as parole and require him to serve it in prison.

The cop came and looked at the trashed hotel lobby. He asked if Peter was drunk. "I had a sip of Heineken," Peter said. "You can test me."

Peter was taken by ambulance to a nearby hospital for evaluation, where he was cleared of drugs and alcohol but had to be booked for criminal mischief. A court date was set.

In court, Peter's lawyer and the judge began negotiating. "Six months in jail," the judge said.

"No," Peter told the lawyer. "I can't do a day. No way. Let's go to trial. They can answer how many fire codes they're breaking by locking a hotel full of people inside."

The judge came back with another offer. "Three months in jail." Peter said no.

Finally, the judge came back with "Three days of community service."

"Deal."

For three days, Peter picked up trash alongside the road for community service. No jail time, no chance that his parole would be violated. Peter actually liked this job. It was outside, and they were given very interesting grabbers that could pick the trash up and drop it in a garbage bag. Peter was picking up trash when he saw a ball of old newspaper. When he picked up the ball, a huge swarm of ground bees attacked him. Peter screamed and ran but the bees followed. They stung his face and his arms and got under his clothes.

The bees finally gave up and went to find what was left of

their hive, leaving Peter Chin covered in welts and bites swelling over most of his body. Peter walked back to the truck where the government supervisor was. The man lifted his head from the newspaper he was reading. "Why you not working no more?"

"Working?" Peter yelled. "Look at me."

The supervisor looked at Peter, whose face was swollen from the bee venom. "Oh. Yeah."

Peter didn't wait to get permission to leave, he just did. "I'm done for the day," he said. "You want to mark me as not here, go ahead."

Peter Chin nursed his bee stings the next day and the next and didn't go back. He had to go back to court. Peter explained about the bees. His lawyer and the judge came to a second deal.

"One day, Mr. Chin," the judge said. "If you serve one day of community service, we can put this issue behind us."

Peter agreed, but there was no way he was going anywhere near where those bees had been.

"They'll send you back to prison," Kenny Wong said, worried. "I'll do it."

The next day, Kenny Wong arrived at the jobsite, signed in as Peter Chin, picked up trash for a day, and the matter was finished.

Peter Chin's parole was saved.

In 2007, with only two years of construction experience and still on federal parole, Peter joined forces with a friend and took on the construction of a new ten-story Ravel Hotel in Long Island City. After this project, Peter built and renovated several New York restaurants.

With his construction knowledge, Peter purchased some properties in the New York area and renovated them to rent out. Then he bought a few more.

Although Peter was building up his businesses, he still had

some technological challenges to work on from being away so long. When Peter went into prison, he communicated by carrying a beeper. When he came out, smartphones and smartwatches were everywhere. One time on the street, Peter saw a man talking on a Bluetooth headpiece, not knowing these existed, only seeing the most well-dressed crazy person he had ever seen talking to himself.

Another time, Peter went into a public bathroom and needed to wash his hands. There were no knobs at the sink. He had just heard the man before him turn on the water, but how? Peter looked under the sink and then pretended to dry his hands as another man came in so he could see how the sink worked. The man put his hands to the sink and the sink turned on, so Peter tried it. Amazing.

Peter borrowed his friend's BMW. He started the car and was about to step outside to smoke a cigarette when he accidentally hit the OnStar button. Seconds later, a bodiless voice, clear and crisp, spoke in the car.

"Do you need help?"

Peter froze but managed to stay calm as he slowly looked in the back seat. Nothing. He opened the car door.

"Is there anything I can do to help you?"

Peter's heart was pounding. He looked under the car, opened the trunk, ran around the car thinking someone was hiding around it.

"Do you need assistance?" the voice repeated.

"Who—" Peter asked. "Who are you?"

"This is OnStar, sir. Do you need us to send you assistance?"

Peter didn't know what OnStar was.

"Assistance?" Peter asked. "Assistance for what?"

Eventually, the OnStar person explained the service they offered and how she was speaking to him and even helped him turn off the OnStar button. Peter understood little of the technology that she'd explained, only that the voice wasn't a ghost and he hadn't lost his mind.

Another time, Peter was in Chinatown and the man in front of him reached for his back pocket to get his phone. Seeing the movement, Peter's instincts told him that this was a hit and the man was getting his pistol out to shoot someone in front of him. Peter threw himself against the wall of the building beside him to get out of the line of fire.

It was a slow adjustment process, but Peter Chin began to adapt to this new world and this new New York. There was still one thing left to do.

The wind was gentle, but it was there. Not a lot, but enough. The trees were far enough apart that they could be avoided if Peter stayed back from them and the wind didn't shift. Peter would have liked to see more wind, maybe be on top of a hill where the wind likes to go, but this flat park worked. This wind would do.

While his sisters set up the picnic at the tables nearby, fifty-six-year-old Peter Chin took the folded kite out of the plastic bag it came in. He unrolled it, looked at the instructions, and began to assemble it.

It wasn't a paper kite like the ones the other kids had in the New Territory outside of Hong Kong, but a plastic kite was still a kite.

Peter connected the cross pieces, tucked them in the small plastic ends, then tied the string to the slit in the flap where a paper grommet would keep it from tearing. He gave himself a bit of slack line like he had seen the other kids do fifty years ago when he was eight years old. He was ready. A promise is a promise, even if you only make it to yourself.

Peter Chin looked behind him. His sisters were smiling and getting ready to videotape him.

"Are you ready?" Peter asked.

They were.

I'm going to fly a kite today, he thought.

And it will be the biggest kite in the sky.

EPILOGUE
By Everett De Morier

If you are ever in Chinatown with Peter Chin, food will mysteriously appear in your hand. You'll be walking, Peter will be talking, and then he'll be gone. You'll notice the silence, then see him come out of some shop and a second later there will be a pastry, kabob, or piece of fried meat on wax paper in your hand. He'll get one for you, one for himself, and you'll move on.

What's interesting about Peter is that knowing how hungry he went in his early life, and what a priority food was in prison, it makes sense that food remains important to him today. This isn't an indulgent need but a connection, an appreciation. If Peter has a bun, he'll tear it and give half to you first. If you are having dinner with him, he will take your plate and start piling different foods on, the biggest and the best portions for you. Food is life, and life is something that needs to be shared.

In preparation for this book, I spent two years getting to know Peter Chin, and we spent the majority of that time talking about his life. Peter has this unique way about him that you can be talking about the intimate details of his life, but you feel that the conversation is all about you. Maybe because he's letting you in, opening that door, but it's easy to feel special when you're around him.

This illuminates the many ironies of Peter Chin. One day

shortly after the agreement for this book was made, while setting up the hotel room for a Zoom call with the literary agent and the publisher, Peter sat back on the couch and said, "I'm going to close my eyes for a second." Minutes later, maybe two minutes tops, I heard the soft snores of a man in deep sleep. He slept hard for twenty minutes, got up refreshed, and we took the Zoom call.

This ability he has to sleep is incredible. I've shared hotel rooms with Peter, and although I'm up and making noise early, there he is, in that restful deep sleep, undisturbed for hours. I've never seen anyone able to fall asleep so fast and so deeply, and for a man who spent part of his life trying not to be assassinated—who used to keep a pistol on the sink next to him while he brushed his teeth—and another part with violent felons, this is even more of an incredible feat.

The other thing worth mentioning is that Peter is by far the best city driver I've ever seen. It's not that he reacts to the traffic around him, but he tends to anticipate what is going to happen moments before it does. Peter will drive us around the small back streets of Chinatown, inches between cars and pedestrians, with almost liquid precision. It's as if he's plugged into the traffic, as if he has insider knowledge of it before it forms around him.

The most recent of Peter's business ventures is a successful hotel chemical business with his business partner. This company provides machines and chemicals for some of the largest hotel chains in New York and Long Island. The vehicle Peter drives is a huge Mercedes cargo van, so big you can stand up in the back, yet he can thread that monster around the narrow and busy streets of Chinatown like a needle through water.

The hotel that Peter was trapped inside and couldn't get buzzed out by the hotel clerk is now one of his hotel chemical clients. Peter goes to the hotel regularly. It no longer has the bulletproof glass.

Another interesting note is that for a man who began learning to read and write English in a prison cell at age twenty-six, Peter has the neatest handwriting I've ever seen.

Since he didn't have a typical childhood, Peter never went fishing for the longest time, though he always wanted to. My son, Alex, and I got to be the ones to take Peter fishing for the very first time. True to the rules of beginner's luck, Peter caught a twelve-inch catfish on his second cast.

At the time of this writing, Peter Chin has been out of prison for twenty years, but he was in prison for twenty-one and a half years, meaning he has still been incarcerated longer than he's been out. If you break down his entire life, Peter spent thirteen years as a kid, another thirteen years on the streets with the Ghost Shadows, twenty-one years incarcerated, and the last twenty years as a free man.

During this time out, Peter has adjusted well, not only to the life outside of prison but to the one beyond the criminal world he once led. He is enthusiastic about life, is always looking for new things to try and experience, and sees the world as an excited twelve-year-old does.

There are still parts of the world that are foreign and even a little frightening to him. Peter uses the internet sparingly and can send an email but would much rather talk over the phone. Making a hotel or a flight reservation online requires outside help. Once, while trying to enter an order number into the comments section of the chemical company's software, Peter deleted the entire company software, which needed to be reinstalled.

Luckily, Peter has developed a strong circle of friends and business partners who are happy to help him.

Through Mike Moy, Peter reconnected with retired Jade Squad detective Neil Mauriello. Peter wrote Neil a letter that Mike read to Neil on his YouTube channel, *Chinatown Gang Stories*, at Neil's home in Florida. My favorite part was this:

Do you remember when you arrested me and you told me that you weren't going to handcuff me but give my dignity and let

*me walk to the 5th Precinct, but if I tried to run, you would
shoot me?*

*You wouldn't have shot me. I know that now. I'm glad I didn't
run, but you wouldn't have shot me.*

Later on, Mike and Peter traveled to Florida to spend a few
days with the former Jade Squad detective, who smiled when
he saw Peter. Neil and Peter stayed in touch and would text
often.

In 2006, through some friends, Peter tracked down Robert
Hsu, a.k.a. Potato. Peter spent an afternoon with Potato at his
home. Peter was happy that Potato was doing so well.

Peter even reconnected with Nicky Louie. After being released from the halfway house and staying at the family's old
apartment, the two men met at a Starbucks in the city and
talked. If you'd walked by, you would have seen two of the most
powerful Dai Los, who had tried to kill each other several
times, sipping coffee.

There were still two people whom Peter couldn't find: Pipenose, the Ghost Shadow who ran into the gambling house with
Peter and guarded it the day the war with Nicky Louie started;
and Monkey, a Ghost Shadow who was part of the RICO indictment with Peter. Monkey had served his time and then Peter
lost track of him.

Life moved on. Peter's chemical business was doing well,
and one day his business partner, Nelson, asked for a favor.

"They need to move a washing machine."

"Who?"

"The family on the third floor. Can you help?"

Sure, Peter would help. They all walked up, Peter was introduced to the father and daughter, and they began maneuver-
ing the washing machine down the steps. While doing this, the
father kept looking at Peter.

The daughter, who knew that Nelson was business partners
with the once famous Kid Jai, was helping guide the washing

machine onto the narrow landing, when her father whispered something to her.

"Walk up to him and call him Kid Jai."

The daughter scowled at her father. "Why would I do that? He's here to help us. Be respectful."

Eventually, as the washing machine made it down to the main floor, the man took his own advice. While they were resting, the man walked over to Peter.

"Kid Jai?" he said.

Peter looked at the man, studied his face.

"Pipenose?" Peter asked. The two men laughed and embraced.

Peter had been looking for Pipenose since coming home, and he lived in the same building as his business partner.

Pipenose had kept his past a secret from his family. His daughter knew that he ran with some people in his youth, but that was it. He never mentioned that he was a Ghost Shadow or that he was part of the pivotal event that changed the leadership of the Ghost Shadows' Mott Street from Nicky Louie to the five generals.

Shortly after the incident where Gene Melvin Jones drank too much and shot up the Ghost Shadows' condo, Peter lost track of his old teacher. I tried to locate him but didn't come up with much outside of a public record of a Gene M. Jones who passed away in 2022 at the age of ninety-four in Florida. There is no written obituary, just a death notice, and since Gene had no family, it's possible that this was him.

On May 10, 2024, retired Detective Neil Mauriello sent Peter a text. Neil had been battling cancer and told Peter that the most recent medical exam was very positive and that Neil had no additional tumors. But on July 1, 2024, Kirk Mauriello, Neil's son, sent a text to Peter from his father's phone stating that Neil was in a coma and was not expected to come out of it. Retired Detective Neil Mauriello passed away later that day.

On August 15, 2022, I received a text from Peter that read: **Call me when you can. Pretty funny.**

I did. I heard Peter Chin, in his car, laughing loudly.

"Did you hear?" he asked.

"No, what?"

"I just heard on the radio. Rudy Giuliani just got charged with"—he allowed a moment to build for dramatic effect—"RICO." He laughed.

"I knew that law would bite him in the ass one of these days."

It wasn't revenge Peter was feeling. It was pure humor. Pure irony. The man who had sent him away for thirty-five years using a law called RICO was now being charged with RICO, forty years later.

This forgiveness Peter possesses is incredibly rare, and I've never seen it in anyone else I've ever come across. Peter has forgiven every last person who ever wronged him, including many who have tried to kill him. He's not only forgiven them, but the wrong is erased, forgotten. With the exception of his father. Peter will never forgive or forget what his father did to his mother and sisters.

The goal of this book was never to canonize Peter Chin, never to glamorize him, but to accurately tell a story that has never been told, by a person who was center stage during a crucial time of Chinatown's history. In doing this over the last two years, I never caught Peter in a lie; I never witnessed him alter a story to make himself look better. His goal of telling the true story far surpassed his need to tell a story where he looked good. Peter's naturally self-deprecating manner guided him.

Peter has been in the United States since he was eight years old. Living in Chinatown, speaking Cantonese for the majority of his life, and being surrounded by Chinese culture, it's almost as if he considers himself a visitor.

One Thanksgiving, I was going away, so we wouldn't be able to work on this book for that entire week.

"Don't worry about it," Peter said. "Thanksgiving is important to Americans. Enjoy and tell Debbie I said hello."

It wasn't said, but it was implied. Thanksgiving is important to *you* Americans. Not meant as a slight, not meant to be disrespectful. Because that's not Peter. He was demonstrating that his world is different from mine. The Asian American world is separate.

Would this book have been different if an Asian writer wrote it? Was it selfish for me to not step aside to let someone from Peter's culture and background tell his story? Maybe.

But then I wouldn't have been able to present it to you with a naïve but fascinated perspective, and most importantly, to see the world through Peter, a man who had fewer chances and advantages than I did but used what he was given in the way he thought was best.

As selfish as that may be—I think I'll keep that.

At the time of this writing, four of the twenty-five Ghost Shadows indicted in 1985 in the RICO case are still fugitives. To protect their anonymity, we won't mention their real or street names here.

The fortune teller that Stinky Bug and Peter met with in 1979 said that Peter's second hurdle, the one that will be harder to overcome than when Peter was shot in 1980, will happen when Peter turns seventy-two. At the time of this writing, this is six years away for Peter Chin, in the year 2031.

It is my personal hope that this fortune teller was completely full of shit.

Q & A with Peter Chin

Q: You had a well-known writer approach you while you were in prison to tell your story, but you didn't do it. Why?

A: It was too painful to talk about my childhood and he wanted to do it while I was inside. If I wanted to tell this story, I wanted it done the right way, not just a few interviews from prison. But I never thought my story was all that interesting, that important.

Q: But when you got out, you decided it was time to tell your story. Why?

A: The only reason this book happened was Mike Moy. He convinced me that if this book could help one person, then I had to do it. And he said all this about preserving the history of Chinatown and I thought this was all talk, until we became friends and I saw that's what he really wanted to do.

Q: What was the hardest part about going through all of this and reliving it again?

A: Remembering certain things. I remember I was probably ten years old, we were in the United States by then, on East Broadway. I was on the top bunk and Mary was on the one below and something woke me up. I looked out and my mom was kneeling on the floor in some kind of Chinese worship. There was a candle lit and a statue of Buddha or some god, I can't remember which one, and she had on this pink dress. I never seen this dress before, she must have brought it with her from Hong Kong, it was like a gala dress, from when she was young.

I looked down on my mom. She was crying but she wasn't crying; she was crying without sound, you know, not wanting to wake nobody up. I get down and see that there is a knife on the floor. I went and grabbed Mary and told her, "Something's happening, something's happening," and Mary got up and we went to our mom. Even as little as I was, I knew my mom was trying to commit suicide, I knew and then I started crying and screaming at her. "How can you be so cruel," I said. "How can you be so cruel to leave us with him?" And then she was crying and was holding my mother and just repeating, "We only have you. That's all we got. We only have you."

Q: Wow, you never told me that story before.

A: I loved my mother. She didn't take a vacation, she never went to the salon, all her clothes she made, she only worked and took care of us. It's funny that when I first left home at thirteen, eating that bread and sleeping with the rats, I was happier then when I was in that apartment with him.

Q: It must have been bad.

A: If my father walked into a room, everyone walked out. I was afraid to cough when he was there. I used to hold coughs in. When I was on the streets, I met some mean people there and in prison—killers, bad guys—but the meanest and cruelest gangster I ever met has nothing next to my father.

Q: I spoke to your sister the other day and she said that she has forgiven your father. If I could push a button and you could forgive him, would you?

A: No. I don't hold anger anymore, but I can never forgive my father for what he did to my mother and my sisters. Never.

Q: Are you happy with the way the book turned out?

A: Yeah, you did a good job. My thing was that if I was going to do this, I was going to do it right and make sure it was accurate and true. If something happened and I was there, I say it. If I wasn't there, then I don't say it. But I wouldn't do it again.

Q: Why?

A: Too painful to go through again. I'm glad we did it, but I'm glad it's over.

Q: There are about five Ghost Shadows whose names we leave out because they are still fugitives from the RICO in 1984. If they were to read this, what would you like to say to them?

A: They know who they are and I wish them well. It would be nice to see them again, but hey, I get it. They have another life now.

ACKNOWLEDGMENTS

We would like to acknowledge the following people for their help and hard work in making this book possible:

Mike Moy, for his pursuit and friendship of Peter Chin and for his devotion to protecting the criminal history of Chinatown.

Literary agent Tina Wainscott, who saw the potential of this project and then used all her skills to find the right home for it.

James Abbate, editor at Kensington Publishing, who carried this project ahead with the dignity and respect that it deserved.